MANAGEMENT
METHODS

Derek Torrington

Jane Weightman

Kirsty Johns

Institute of Personnel Management

British Library Cataloguing in Publication Data
Torrington, Derek
    Management methods.
    1. Management
    I. Title   II.   Weightman, Jane   III.   Johns, Kirsty
    658.4   HD31

    ISBN 0-85292-355-4

ISBN 0 85292 355 4

First published 1985

Typeset by Illustrated Arts Ltd. Surrey, and
Printed in Great Britain by Dotesios Limited, Bradford-on-Avon.

Contents

1 *Introduction*   *vii*

A   Personal organization and effectiveness

2   Management work   *3*
3   Analyzing your own job   *7*
4   Personal organization   *11*
5   Interpersonal communication   *15*
6   Assertiveness   *19*
7   Negotiating and influencing   *23*
8   Problem-solving   *27*
9   Report-writing   *31*
10 Reading   *35*
11 Coping with stress   *39*

B   Working in the organization

12 Forms of organization   *45*
13 Organizational politics   *49*
14 Knowing your own organizational system   *53*
15 Dealing with problems of organization   *57*
16 Analyzing your network of contacts   *61*
17 Organizational communication   *65*
18 Group-working   *69*
19 Analysis of team roles   *73*
20 Committees   *77*
21 Dealing with change   *81*

C   Managing people

22 Departmental organization   *87*
23 Job design   *91*
24 Understanding other people   *95*
25 Power and authority   *99*

26 Procedures for mutual control   103
27 Staff selection   107
28 Counselling and coaching   111
29 Dealing with the poor performer   115
30 Performance appraisal   119
31 Brainstorming   123

D Administrative Action

32 Procedures for administrative action   129
33 Goal planning and setting objectives   133
34 Decision-making   137
35 Job analysis   141
36 Critical path analysis   145
37 Linear programming   149
38 Computer systems   153
39 Information storage and location   157
40 Project analysis and investment appraisal   161
41 Activity scheduling   165

E Monitoring

42 Comparing performance with plan   171
43 Trends and predictions   175
44 Departmental budgetary control   179
45 Sampling methods   183
46 Graphs and diagrams   187
47 Personnel indicators   191
48 Depreciation   195
49 Cash flow   199
50 Reading the balance sheet   203
51 Productivity measures   207

1 Introduction

We will begin by saying what sort of a person we think you, the reader, are likely to be. You may be very experienced and effective, or you may be new to a management post, but you will believe you could do it better with more know-how. If you already know all there is to know about managing, you had better lend this book to someone else. If you are unsure about whether or not you want to be in management in the first place, you will need a different book, because we include very little discussion of issues; rather, we concentrate on methods of doing things.

We believe you are a manager who does not yet know all the answers. We believe also that you do not like reading management books. You are busy, with little time and patience for extended, thoughtful discussion on the issue of management. To you management is action, getting things done and tackling problems as they present themselves, while reading books is passive and reflective. You will read reports and memoranda, and will read the odd article in a management journal, but reading books and doing the job of management will seem to you activities that sit uneasily together.

If we have so far given a fairly accurate description of yourself, we suggest you read the rest of this introductory chapter to see if this book can be of use to you.

In working out our ideas we have given this book two complementary nicknames: 'brief case book' and 'cookery book'. We regard it as a brief case book because we hope you will put it in your brief-case to read bit by bit while on trains or waiting at airports, or to look up something when going through figures or before attending a meeting. We do not expect you to sit down and read it from start to finish. It is designed to be read spasmodically, without the risk of losing the thread of any argument.

The term 'cookery book' is usually a term of abuse among management academics for texts that tell people how to do things, but we hope we have avoided the pitfall of being trite by providing solid and compact explanations of why methods should work as well as how to work them. The main content is recipes for dealing with practical events, from the relatively straightforward task of report writing to the mysteries of dealing with organizational politics, the subtleties of counselling and the statistical precision of sampling methods.

The methods are presented in self contained units and you may choose to start almost anywhere, depending on the exigencies of your job. For example, if you have to chair a committee for the first time, we suggest reading chapter 20 a few days beforehand, with a final glance through the chapter 10 minutes before the meeting begins; if you feel that things are getting out of hand and there is too much to do, have a look at chapter 4; if you need to make a presentation of complex information to a group of shop stewards, overseas customers or local politicians, see if you find any help in chapter 46, or chapter 5, or perhaps chapter 6; if you are puzzled by some aspect of how your organization works, try reading chapters 12 to 16 inclusive. Incidentally, if you are *not* puzzled by some aspect of how your organization works please let us know: you must be unique.

Fifty aspects of management are presented in the following common format of four pages:

Page 1 Background explanation and comment on the method to be described.

Pages 2 Brief explanatory material featuring, for example, check lists, and 3 guidance notes, drills and procedures, methods of analysis, statistical techniques and sample documents.

Page 4 Practical exercises, suggestions for further reading, and a final word on the topic.

The topics are arranged in five parts:
A   Personal organization and effectiveness
B   Working in the organization
C   Managing people
D   Administrative action
E   Monitoring

In all our discussions with managers we have found that they worry about how well organized they are personally, and that the key to their greater efficiency and peace of mind is usually the resolution of some minor, persistent anxiety relating to personal effectiveness. Next, comes the problem of working in an organization, understanding how it functions and coming to terms with the fact that it is a mess. This is not a cynical view. As implied earlier, we have not found anyone who does not regard their organization as in some way unsatisfactory, and nearly all the managers we have spoken to believe their organizations work badly. The puzzle is that they all believe that organizations should work perfectly. When they stop worrying and accept that malfunctioning establishments can still function and make a decent return on investment, they improve their own personal management performance.

It would be easy to think that managing people is the manager's greatest problem. Our investigations suggest that managers who are reasonably well organized and who understand the working of the relevant organization have fewer problems in managing people. This is because their own problems are not a hindrance to their dealings with others. Nonetheless, there are still a range of jobs to be done in managing people, and these are covered in the third grouping of topics.

The fourth and fifth parts of the book are a suggested series of ways in which administrative action takes place, followed by methods of monitoring the performance of relevant sections or departments so that the manager is aware of what is happening and can decide whether it is going well or badly.

We have sought to combine an academic study of management processes with our own personal experiences of managerial work and the working environment. The main basis of what we are writing is our extensive reading in the management literature and detailed research among managers in a large number of very different organizations. This is reinforced and put into perspective by extensive working experience in areas as diverse as engineering, education, banking and the oil and chemical industries.

We believe the methods we describe will work in most real life situations. They may not be precisely correct for your particular situation, but they should be sufficient as guidelines to provide a practical, and not simply a theoretical, basis for action.

A   Personal organization and effectiveness

Some managers find that their biggest enemies are themselves, as they never get on top of the job, are not clear on how to set about the various aspects of what they have to do, and have difficulties in their working relationships.

The following 10 chapters are intended to help you to avoid those sorts of problems. First we explain some of the ways in which management jobs differ and the basic methods used by managers in their work. These are followed by methods of job analysis for the reader in order to see how the different components are balanced and the choices available to improve the degree of control exercised. The subsequent three chapters cover personal dealings with people, from the basic elements of interpersonal communication to techniques in the development of assertiveness and self confidence, and the specialized skills of negotiating with groups or influencing individuals. Three quite different aspects of personal method are described in the final three chapters: not the social skills of dealing with other people, but the rational skills of finding the best way through a problem, writing reports that not only say what you want to say but also get read and implemented, and developing methods of reading which discriminate between reading for information, understanding and criticism. This section of the book concludes with some methods of understanding stress and coping with this particular aspect of management life.

Any manager who masters the skills and techniques described will become markedly more effective, not only in the job, but also in many other aspects of living.

2　Management work

The work of managers has been defined traditionally as the art of getting things done through people, but this is not limited to managers. All those who organize human affairs have management work to do. Teachers, orchestral conductors, parents, ambassadors, chefs, bishops, senior systems analysts and many others all have a management ingredient to their jobs, but they are less likely to emphasize it and may not even recognise it. It is not the purpose of the jobs, but a feature of their jobs that has to get done.

The work of managers has been studied carefully in the last 30 years and it will be no surprise to managers reading this book that most studies show the manager's day to be characterized by constant interruptions, brief periods of specialized activity and constant switching from one task to another. Management work is not a serene activity of continuous, thoughtful planning and assimilation of reports. There is constant change, and most managers spend between 50 and 80 per cent of their time talking to other people.

Kotter (1982) gives a useful definition of the core behaviours of managers as that of first setting agendas for action and then establishing and maintaining networks to implement those agendas. Agendas are lists of things to be done, written down or remembered, thought out or vague, short term or long term. These come about by generating possibilities, questioning plans and proposals, gathering information and calculating ways and means of implementing policies, plans, strategies and agreements. These agendas are implemented through a network of contacts the manager builds up, not only direct subordinates and close colleagues. This is dealt with further in chapters 16 and 17 and a more detailed analysis of management work is shown overleaf.

The nature of management work varies with the job. Differentiation by function groups together those activities that are associated with production, marketing, personnel or some other functional division of the management process, so that the grouping and identification of the managers is according to their specialist expertise. Management work also varies with level in the hierarchy. Top managers are those at the apex of the organizational pyramid, like a board of directors, who have few but vital responsibilities concerning the overall direction of the business, like merger, acquisition and closure. Senior managers are concerned with policy formulation and implementation. The initial stages of implementation are likely to produce major problems and queries, and this is the main reason why the lives of senior managers tend to be frenetic. Middle managers complete the process of implementation within the organization and try to resolve the unintended consequences of the policies themselves. Supervisory managers arrange for the work for which the organization exists to be done: making cars, running the sales office, producing ice cream, making up hotel beds and so forth, in other words dealing with the day to day variations and demands.

These varying ways of describing management work help us to develop an understanding of it. The next two pages take the analysis further.

The 10 roles of the manager

Formal authority
and status ⟶

INTERPERSONAL ROLES

1 *Figurehead*, to represent the unit formally
2 *Liaison*, to deal with peers and outsiders in order to swap information
3 *Leader*, to staff the unit and motivate its members

INFORMATIONAL ROLES

4 *Monitor*, to gather and store information useful to the unit
5 *Disseminator*, to pass on to subordinates information not otherwise available
6 *Spokesperson*, to pass information out from the unit

DECISIONAL ROLES

7 *Entrepreneur*, to initiate change
8 *Disturbance handler*, to take charge when the unit is threatened
9 *Resource allocator*, to decide where and how unit resources will be deployed
10 *Negotiator*, to deal with outsiders whose consent and cooperation is required by the unit

The composition of the manager's incoming mail

	%
Reports on operations	18
Periodical news	15
Reference data	14
Status requests	12
General reports	8
Events	8
Advice on situations	6
Solicitations	5
Authority requests	5
Acknowledgements	5
Ideas	2
Problems and pressures	2

Distribution of hours and activities in the chief executive's work

Hours spent

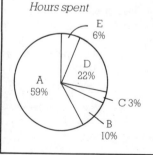

Number of activities

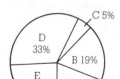

A   Scheduled meetings

B   Unscheduled meetings

C   Tours

D   Desk work

E   Telephone calls

An alternative method of classifying management jobs

HUB jobs have necessary contact with subordinates, superiors and peers. It is the most common type of job and has a dominant human management component.

PEER DEPENDENT jobs are those with less 'vertical' demand and much dependence on winning the cooperation of peers. Often found on the boundaries of organizations.

MAN MANAGEMENT jobs are those concerned primarily with the vertical type of working relationship, having contact mainly with superiors and subordinates.

SOLO jobs are those of managers who spend a large part of their time working alone on assignments.

The gods of management

A more whimsical idea is that there are four gods of management that embody the philosophy, culture and structure of organizations or parts of organizations. Each person will have a preferred god, but each of the four can be useful in particular circumstances.

ZEUS The god of the club culture with a central figure, as in a spider's web. The mode of dynamic entrepreneurs who rule their empires on snap decisions.

APOLLO The god of the role culture, with everyone in their proper place doing prescribed jobs. The bureaucratic order often found in large organizations.

ATHENA The goddess of the task culture, where expertise is the basis of power and influence. The matrix structure.

DIONYSUS The god of the existential culture where role is based on personal relations without a defined boss. Found as a form of organizations among artists and some professionals.

Sources

The material on the facing page is adapted from the work of Henry Mintzberg, the material on this page is taken from the books of Rosemary Stewart and Charles Handy. Mintzberg's conclusions are based mainly on a detailed study of the work of chief executives. Stewart studied the work of 252 more varied job holders.

Exercises

1 Which god do you serve? Which does your boss believe in? How would you convert the boss to your view?

2 What is your agenda at the moment? Who is going to help you to achieve these things?

3 Michael Edwardes argues (1984) "It is better to have a focal point of leadership which is crisp and sharp, than to wallow in consensus, which we do in Britain." Which god does this fit in with?

Further reading

EDWARDES M. in 'UK Squanders its Management Talent' in *Chief Executive*. Nov. 1984 pp 10–15

HANDY C. *The Gods of Management*. London, Pan, 1978

KOTTER J. *The General Managers*. New York, The Free Press, 1982

MINTZBERG H. *The Nature of Managerial Work*. New York, Harper and Row, 1973

MINTZBERG H. 'The Manager's Job: Folklore and Fact' in *Harvard Business Review*. July/Aug 1975, p 49

STEWART R. *Managers and Their Jobs*. London, Macmillan, 1967

STEWART R. *Contrasts in Management*. Maidenhead, Berks., McGraw-Hill, 1976

MANT A. *The Rise and Fall of the British Manager*. London, Macmillan, 1977

And finally . . .

In understanding managerial work we must remember:
    "Management is a much less tidy, less organised, and less easily defined activity than that traditionally presented by management writers or in job descriptions."

Stewart, R., 1976. p125

3 Analyzing your own job

Analyzing your own job can help you do it better by showing up the opportunities you are missing and the difficulties you are not overcoming. Our method is to distinguish between three types of work that managers do: technical, administrative and managerial, and consider the balance between the three.

Technical work is what managers do because of their profession, experience or qualification. This kind of work is often done also by subordinates, and is the sort of work the manager did before being promoted to management. A manager is doing technical work when, for instance, a sales manager negotiates with a customer, when a senior nursing officer nurses a patient, or a hotel manager books in a client. Technical work is usually concerned with the main task of the unit or organization.

Administrative work of managers is that concerned with organizational maintenance. It is work concerned with carrying out official, often regular duties, authorized by others, such as a boss or a committee. Managers are doing administrative work when, for instance, they work out the hours worked by subordinates, check expenses or fill in weekly returns.

Managerial work is that of conducting organizational affairs with the freedom to create precedents. Managers are doing managerial work when they persuade others to agree to a new line of action, when they take risky decisions, or get people to do things they would not otherwise have done.

Managers' jobs vary in the balance between these three types of work that are present. This is partly due to function, and to level in the hierarchy, but also because of the choices made by individual managers. Rosemary Stewart (1982) has shown that the differences between management jobs can be understood by looking at the demands, constraints and choices of a job to see how effectively it is being done.

Demands can be defined as meeting the minimum criteria of performance and specific work that has to be done. Constraints limit a manager's choices by defining what, where and how the work is to be done. Then, however, there are choices in what and how the work is done. By analyzing your job with the method shown overleaf, you can see what choices you are making and can see how that range can be extended to give you more positive control over the choices, rather than assuming that all work is dictated by others.

Managers abandon their technical work too easily in favour of administrative work. If they exercise more of their choices to maintain their technical skills, they keep in touch with the main task of the organization, have the satisfaction of using their technical skills, and are more likely to survive in times of company reorganization. Technical skills are readily transferable to different situations, but administrative skills are usually relevant only in the organizational context in which they have been acquired.

How much managerial work does your job include?

Record how you spend your time at work for at least one day. A suggested format is set out below. Try to do it during the day in question and not later, so that you do not forget the small details. Every time you change an activity, start a new line. A change of activity is either moving to a new topic or a new person. Meetings count as one activity. Tick how the activity was initiated, how it was conducted and which of the broad category of skills was involved, as defined on the previous page.

		Initiative		Method			Type of work		
Time	Activity	Self	Other	Face to face	Phone	Alone	Tech	Admin	Managerial

The information collected in these sheets can be used in various ways, including those suggested in the next chapter. Does your day fit that described in the last chapter as typical, with constant interruptions and only brief periods on any one topic? Are you surprised about the time distribution? How much of your day was spent responding to others? How much of your day was spent with other people? What proportion of your day was spent using technical skills, what proportion using administrative skills and what proportion using managerial skills? Is that distribution acceptable to you? See if you can get greater control over your affairs by using the checklist on the facing page.

What choices do you have at work?

The choices you have at work are restricted by the demands and constraints of your job. However, every job has some choices. You can analyze the choices available to you by looking at the following questions.

Demands

What are the demands of your job? That is the things that have to be done by you. They cannot be ignored, delegated or passed on. What are the penalties for not doing them? It might help to think of the following areas:

1   Subordinates
2   More senior members of staff
3   Peers
4   People outside the organization
5   Administration – procedures and meetings
6   Others

Constraints

What are the constraints that stop you developing your job in absolutely the way you would like? For example:

1   The resources, eg buildings
2   Legal or trade union
3   Technical limitations of equipment
4   Physical location
5   Organization policies and procedures
6   Attitude of others
7   Other

Choices

There are choices about *what* you do, *how* you do it and *when* you do it. What are the choices available to you?

1   Within your unit
2   With your peers
3   To protect the unit from disturbance
4   Upwards
5   Elsewhere in the organization
6   Outside the organization
7   Other

Based on the work of R. Stewart, *Choices for the Manager, op cit*

Exercises

1 Using the drills on the last two pages, compare your job with that of a colleague doing similar work. How different are your balances between technical, administrative and managerial work? What causes these differences? Are there ways in which you can exercise a greater degree of choice in your job?

2 Listed at the foot of the page are some advantages and disadvantages of technical, administrative and managerial work. Can you think of any more?

Further reading

TORRINGTON D P and WEIGHTMAN J B. 'Technical Atrophy in Middle Management' in *Journal of General Management*. 1982, vol. 8, no. 4

STEWART R. *Choices for the Manager*. Maidenhead, Berks., McGraw-Hill, 1982

And finally . . .

The balance of work for managers:

	Technical	Administrative	Managerial
Advantages	Authority of expertize Keep in touch with subordinates' work Pride in work Task-oriented	Easy to do Even pace Keeps things running smoothly	React quickly to differences between plan and reality Make choices and decisions
Disadvantages	Lose sight of overall aims of organization 'Generalist' skills not developed Subordinates may be denied scope if technical workload limited	Subordinates irked by demands Comfort of doing something certain creates more administrative work Administrative work can become an end in itself	Hectic pace Erratic demands Lot of time spent building networks, which can become more important than getting the job done.

4 Personal organization

Personal organization is about managing oneself effectively. By controlling one's work consciously one becomes more aware of the choices to be made and consequently less passive. Personal organization is deciding what, how, where, when and with whom it needs doing. Why something is done is often dictated by others, the boss, committee, customer or colleagues and is less a question of personal organization.

Memory is frequently mentioned by busy managers as being worse than it used to be. It is hardly surprising in a constantly interrupted, disjointed day that some facts and opinions are not recalled unless jotted down. Junior employees usually work for long periods on single tasks and so have more opportunity to store and rehearse the information relevant to the job. No training programme would ever organize information input to be constantly interrupted in the way of much of the manager's input. Thus, the only way to remember much in these circumstances is to organize consciously.

Time is often seen to be in short supply by managers. There are several different aspects to this. Where a large number of different demands are made on a manager's time, priorities need to be set and some demands will have to be deferred or refused. Finding longer periods of time for collecting and organizing information, report writing and longer term projects is difficult to maintain when immediate demands are made which can be resolved immediately. Some claims of pressure of time can be attributed to a lack of desire to do something.

Keeping the paperwork under control is important. Many organizations have papers copied for large numbers of people partly to prevent the excuse of not being informed, and partly to maintain the political network. Consequently, most managers' in-tray will contain more papers than are strictly necessary to get the job done. Add to this the comfort to be gained from doing something where the end is achievable, such as emptying the in-tray, and paperwork can take up a disproportionate amount of time and energy. The art is in keeping the paper organized.

One of the choices that managers cherish and protect is the right to control their own diaries. This can develop sometimes into a demonstration of relative status and power when trying to agree dates. Having decided when to meet, and with whom, the place for the meeting will be dictated by relative status and convenience. If you get the other person to come to you, less of your time is consumed, but the other person will have slightly more control over the time the meeting finishes.

The poorly organized manager responds to the initiatives of other people, and is dependent on them. A lack of preparation enables others to dominate, slows things down, produces errors and leads to dissatisfaction. Indications of this are such phrases as "I've just not had the time", "Let's play this one by ear", "I'm still waiting for ...", "I've tried to contact them but ...", "I'm sorry I quite forgot about it".

Memory

There are different types of memory. The main sorts are:

Recall, which is being able to repeat the task, message, behaviour, without referring to notes. This type of memory is not always as accurate as we think.

Recognition, is being able to recognize or distinguish that the material is familiar. For example, when we look in the file and remember the problem we were having with the order from a supplier.

Improved assimilation, is the act of not recognizing something as familiar but understanding or learning much more quickly than the first time the material was encountered.

What level of memory is necessary? A lot of management work can be at the recognition level. For example, notes are consulted, the matter is dealt with and then forgotten.

Ways of improving recall. Rehearse the material at the start. For example, repeat the name of the person you have just been introduced to. Practising helps memory.

Ways of improving recognition. Keep an action list of what needs doing. Next to appointments in your diary put the topic to be discussed.

Time

Decide what the priorities are.
What *must* you do today, this week, this month, this year?
What *should* you do today, this week, this month, this year?
What do you *hope* to do today, this week, this month, this year?
What can be ignored, passed 'up', delegated 'down'?

Setting a pattern for the day can marshal time effectively, for example:

Taking phone calls 9–11
Making telephone calls 2–4
Signing expense claims and letters 4:30–5

This patterning can also work for the week.

Paperwork

Filing   Current material is usually in one folder, briefcase or tray. Most filing cabinets have a few, bulging files and a larger number that are almost empty. A list of files can spread usage, because managers will then consult the list to find documents instead of relying on only those few files they can recall. Most file titles are by source, such as a file for each customer, or by use, such as a file for each committee.
The 'just in case I should ever need it' can probably be thrown away, especially if it is likely to be retained in someone else's filing cabinet.

Bring out systems   are files by date, so that material is filed for review on a predetermined date, thereby avoiding pressure on the bulging current file and avoiding the risk of the matter being overlooked.

Colour coding   is a way of sorting paper, by using different colours for different purposes, with white for advice, pink for information and red for action. This usually fails because of the tendency for all memoranda soon to be typed on red paper!

There are a number of products on the market that provide a simple organizing element for the manager, eg organizer diaries and the 'Filofax' system of small files with sheets to cover a variety of situations.

Diaries

Mark preparation periods, for example before an important meeting mark three days previously 'prepare for . . . meeting'.

Mark recurring items, for example last Tuesday of every month 'returns in'.

Give talkative people an appointment just before lunch or a meeting so you both have an incentive to stop.

Remember travelling time.

If you are running very late why not phone and say so?

Exercises

1 Have a look in the filing cabinet and count how many files you have used in the last week. How many have you not used in the last year?

2 When you are introduced to new people try saying their name eg 'How nice to meet you Mrs . . . .'.

3 Look at your action list – make one if you don't already have one – and mark it for 'must', 'should' and 'hope' for the next week.

4 Practise delegating both up and down, saving for yourself that work which only you can do.

5 If you were able to organize yourself better who would benefit?

6 List five ways in which you manage your boss. Could these be improved?

Further reading

BOURSINE D P and GUERRIER Y. *Surviving as a Middle Manager*. Beckenham, Kent, Croom Helm, 1983

BUZAN T. *How to Make the Most of Your Mind*. London, Colt Books, 1977

PEDLER M, BURGOYNE J and BOYDELL T. *A Manager's Guide to Self Development*. Maidenhead, Berks., McGraw-Hill, 1978

And finally . . .

Personal organization also means looking after one's own interests. One way is to consider one's goals for the future; personal, social, material and career. If these goals are different from where one is now, what can be done about it? One technique for career goals in management has been the development of programmes of self development to increase skills and knowledge.

5 Interpersonal communication

Interpersonal communication is used here to describe the one to one or small group conversations in which managers spend most of their time. Effectiveness in these situations is one of the keys to successful management performance, as this is how managers get things done: a person is persuaded to follow a new invoice procedure, the logic of a new marketing plan is explained and justified, a problem is eased or enthusiasm engendered. There are briefing sessions and the everyday conversations for social contact and stimulation that maintain smooth cooperative and personal relations. Each of these requires some variation of the manager's personal communications style and difficulties can arise if these varying demands are not understood.

Communication is a two-way process, complete only when the message is received and understood, even if the understanding is not exactly what was intended. Both the sender and receiver of a message have an active part to play. This reciprocal process is sometimes described as the speech chain and uses systems or information theory terms to describe the process. For effective communication to take place each of the following six stages needs to be operating well; encoding, transmitting, environment, receiving, decoding and feedback (see overleaf). When we want to be effective communicators we need to consider not only our own performance but also with whom we are communicating, and the likely effect of what we are saying and how we are saying it. To consider whom we are conversing with we need to understand them. This is dealt with in more detail in chapter 24. Understanding other people is difficult because we all have a set of operating assumptions to conduct our daily lives by, and we all have a different set. If we do not recognize this diversity, communication becomes at best awkward and at worst non-existent.

Factors other than those involved in the communication can also effect the outcome of a conversation or meeting. Physical factors such as noise and temperature are obvious factors. The position of the furniture can also play a part. Seating a group so they can all see each other increases interaction. Having a table between participants increases the formality but gives them quite literally something to hold on to if it is a tense situation. Interruptions from the telephone or keeping an 'open door' disrupt communication.

Difficulties can occur because the purpose of the communication is unclear, problems in the speech chain, or outside factors. Where effective communication is critical each stage needs to be considered in order to preempt any possible problems.

Methods of Interpersonal Communication

1 Getting started

Establish rapport, so that participants get used to each others' tone, volume and personality.

Methods include: small talk, friendly manner, calm attention and explaining what is going to happen.

2 Keeping it going

Maintain rapport and keep the communication to the agenda.

Methods include: showing interest, giving verbal and non-verbal signals of agreement, making encouraging noises but keeping silent at times when other people are considering points. It may sometimes be necessary to bring suppressed feelings into the open by asking a question like 'Is there something on your mind . . . ?'

3 Questions

There are different types of question according to what you want to do:

Type	Purpose	Example
Closed	To seek precise information	'What is your name?'
Open	To get opinions developed	'How do you do that?'
Direct	To insist on a reply	'Why did you do that?'
Indirect	An oblique approach to a difficult matter	'What were they like?'
Probe	To obtain information that is being withheld. One way is to exaggerate	'You weren't in prison, were you?'
Proposing	To put forward an idea	'Shall we do as Tom suggests?'
Rhetorical	To forbid a reply	'We're not afraid of the competition, are we?'

4 Stopping

Slow the general rate of talking by slipping one or two closed questions into the conversation and eliminating encouraging gestures.

Gather your papers together and say something to indicate closing, such as 'Well, I think we have covered the ground . . .'

Explain the next step, such as who does what.

Stand up.

The basic communications model or speech chain

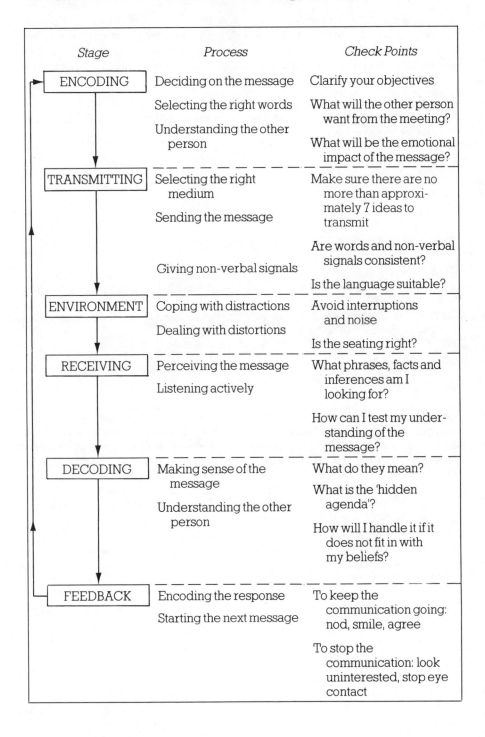

Stage	Process	Check Points
ENCODING	Deciding on the message	Clarify your objectives
	Selecting the right words	What will the other person want from the meeting?
	Understanding the other person	What will be the emotional impact of the message?
TRANSMITTING	Selecting the right medium	Make sure there are no more than approximately 7 ideas to transmit
	Sending the message	
		Are words and non-verbal signals consistent?
	Giving non-verbal signals	Is the language suitable?
ENVIRONMENT	Coping with distractions	Avoid interruptions and noise
	Dealing with distortions	Is the seating right?
RECEIVING	Perceiving the message	What phrases, facts and inferences am I looking for?
	Listening actively	
		How can I test my understanding of the message?
DECODING	Making sense of the message	What do they mean?
		What is the 'hidden agenda'?
	Understanding the other person	How will I handle it if it does not fit in with my beliefs?
FEEDBACK	Encoding the response	To keep the communication going: nod, smile, agree
	Starting the next message	
		To stop the communication: look uninterested, stop eye contact

Exercises

1 From a group of people ask two to leave the room to prepare a brief talk on their present occupations. Agree with the rest of the group to give positive feedback to the first and negative feedback to the second. Ask the two speakers to come in one at a time and give their talks. Discuss the reactions of the speakers and the audience's behaviour.

2 Which of the following seating arrangements do you think would be most appropriate for a counselling session, a union negotiation and a selection interview? Give your reasons.

Further reading

Torrington D P. *Face to Face in Management*. London, Prentice Hall, 1982

Goffman E. *The Presentation of Self in Everyday Life*. Harmondsworth, Middx., Penguin, 1972

Argyle M. *The Psychology of Interpersonal Behaviour*. Harmondsworth, Middx., Pelican, 1972

Berne E. *Games People Play*. London, Andre Deutsch, 1966

And finally . . .

Berne has made an interesting analysis of how we interact with each other. He proposes that each of us has within us behaviours that can be described as Parent, Adult or Child. When we communicate with others all combinations are possible. Two of the more common are:

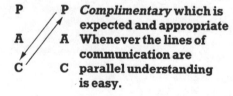 *Complimentary* which is expected and appropriate Whenever the lines of communication are parallel understanding is easy.

 Crossed where the first statement gets an inappropriate response from the other person

6 Assertiveness

A contemporary phobia is the fear of being pushed around. Some people are nervously afraid of queue-jumpers, for example; others live in dread of being put down by waiters or taxi drivers. Managers have to avoid being pushed around. They have to assert themselves in situations and obtain the attention for their projects that is required for them to succeed.

A useful definition of assertiveness is:

> Self-expression through which one stands up for one's basic human rights without violating the basic human rights of others.
>
> Kelley, 1979, p. 14

There is an underlying assumption that assertiveness can be learned: there are no assertive people, only people who have learned how to assert themselves. Also it is not to be confused with aggression or abrasiveness, which are usually indicators that a person does not have the self confidence to be assertive.

The need for assertiveness is partly a product of overcrowding. When people are crowded together, either literally in a rush hour bus or metaphorically in a busy organization, they get in each other's way, the individual finds it difficult to establish personal space and privacy, the weak are inhibited by the strong and all compete with each other for recognition, identity and achievement. When an organization is short of opportunities for its people to achieve their ambitions, there is a need for individuals to be assertive to maintain their self esteem, but not to be aggressive and weaken the self esteem of others.

The easiest way to distinguish assertiveness is to see it as a middle position between diffidence and aggression. Diffident people allow themselves to be trodden on, being anxious not to offend. They will feel badly about this behaviour, but will internalize the feeling as part of the diffident façade that is to be presented. Aggressive people express their feelings, which are of anger or outrage, in ways that offend or antagonize the people they are dealing with. Assertive people express their feelings, but in ways that are socially acceptable and that do not make them feel guilty.

In the next chapter there is comment about stroking and transactional analysis. You will see that diffident people have an 'I'm not O.K.: you're O.K.' philosophy, aggressive people demonstrate 'I'm O.K.: you're not O.K.' philosophies and assertive people have 'I'm O.K.: you're O.K.' mentalities.

Self confidence

Each of us develops a self estimate based on what others say about us and on our own assessment of how we measure up to the norms of the society of which we are a part. Poor self estimate comes from concentrating more on our failures than our successes, so that we become preoccupied with what we cannot do (or think we cannot do) rather than what we can.

Self estimate is improved by the drill of rehearsing in one's mind a list of things that are self enhancing: 'I am friendly; I did well at school; I am accurate at calculations; I can make people laugh . . . ' These then can squeeze out thoughts like 'I am fat; I am ugly; I do not express myself well; I am a mess . . . ' Preoccupation with our failures can be self fulfilling, so the shy person who retreats from friendly overtures will probably be judged as stand-offish or disdainful. Concentrating on and amplifying what is good about yourself can also be self fulfilling.

Non-verbal and verbal clues

Diffidence	Assertion	Aggression
Moving from one foot to another	Firm, comfortable stand	Leaning forward stiffly
Backing away from other person	Orienting towards other person	Moving against other person
Wringing hands	Hands relaxed	Clenched fists
Eyes averted or cast down	Eye contact with other person	Glaring, without expression
Voice hesitant or apologetic	Voice steady and clear	Voice staccato and overbearing
Tentative statements: I wonder/would you mind/maybe	Firm statements: I will/I feel/I know/I want	Threats: I'm warning you/ you'd better
Negative statements: It doesn't matter/ never mind	Emphatic statements: What do you think/ can you help	Critical statements: This won't do/it's not good enough
Fillers: You know/er/well now/right	Cooperative words: Let's/what can we do/how can we	Sarcasm: You've got to be joking/what makes you think . . .

Thought stopping

Self confidence is undermined by negative thinking, both about oneself gener-ally and in particular situations. Thought stopping is the process of reducing the impact of these negatives by working through a series of challenges to the depressing idea. Here are some examples:

1 'I must be liked or approved of by those around me most of the time.'

Negative effects: Can lose in competitive situations; can give false reassurance to people who need corrective guidance; can be cheated; can resist being angry in situations where anger is needed.

Stoppers: Although it is pleasant to be popular, it is not necessary to be popular with everyone. Doing what you think is right, or needed, is usually better than simply reacting to the demands of others. Taking the side of someone can make you very popular with that person, even if it makes you unpopular with another.

2 'I should never make mistakes.'

Negative effects: Can defer action/can direct attention to detail at expense of main issues/can miss promotion prospects because of feeling unready to apply for challenging jobs.

Stoppers: Although it is satisfying to be perfect, it is not necessary. Being perfect would not make me a better person. Perfection is so difficult to achieve that the desire is seldom satisfied. If a thing is worth doing, it is worth doing badly. Making mistakes can be the best way of improving performance.

Working with other people

1 *Make it easy for other people to do what you want them to do*
Give clear reasons, be sure of your case and ask the right person.

2 *Speak up clearly*
Praise other people, protect your own position, give feedback and be willing to say no.

3 *Define problems and work at them*
When you have difficulty in working with someone, define what the problem is, consider alternative definitions, decide which is correct and work at deal-ing with it.

4 *Recognize the feelings of others*
You are not the only one with problems; neither are you the only one who could be right.

Exercises

1 Describe diffident, assertive and aggressive behaviours in each of the following situations:

   a You have taken an important client to an expensive restaurant for dinner, but there is no trace of your reservation and several other people are waiting too.

   b A colleague has just grumbled about one of your staff members and you feel the comment to be unfair.

   c Your boss rings to say she would like to see you for a meeting in half an hour. You have urgent work to complete and feel that it should take precedence over her meeting.

2 List five aspects of negative thinking that tend to undermine your self confidence and then list some thought stoppers to counteract them.

Further reading

BOWER S A and BOWER G H. *Asserting Yourself: A Practical Guide for Positive Change*. Reading, Mass., Addison Wesley, 1976

KELLEY C. *Assertion Training: A Facilitator's Guide*. San Diego, Calif., University Associates, 1979

And finally ...

Assertive behaviour is always helped by knowing the social system in which you are dealing. Very few people have the confidence to send food back to the kitchen when they are dining in an expensive restaurant for example, yet frequently waiters will be potential allies. They have loyalty to you, the customer, from whom they expect a tip, as well as to the restaurant in general and the chef in particular. Have you ever seen a waiter refuse to take an underdone steak back to the kitchen? Also consider the sweet trolley. This is completely under the control of the waiter, and not the chef. The waiter wants your approval in order to get a tip: they will *always* give you a second helping.

7 Negotiating and influencing

In dealing with other people you cannot always get what you want. You may get less, but you could also get more than you had expected, or even more than you had thought of. Managers spend much of their time negotiating with customers, suppliers, employees, and each other: doing deals. Some people dislike this activity, as it smacks of uncertainty, unsatisfactory compromise, fudge and bribery. The Americanism 'wheeling and dealing' implies that you will turn in almost any direction to reach a bargain, and for some people the process of dealing can become more important than the objective at the start of the process.

There are many situations, however, that require negotiation and one of the best outcomes is where the parties both emerge from the encounter with more than they had thought of: the process of negotiating can reveal possibilities of mutual advantage that neither party individually could contemplate. In this way, your adversary becomes your helper.

Negotiations take place only when the parties need each other. The buyer needs the seller, the research manager needs the cooperation of the engineering manager, the armaments supplier needs the arms user, so that in each situation both parties know that they can 'win' only if the other person is not beaten. One of the informal aspects of negotiation is the convention of 'shaking hands on it', implying that both parties are satisfied with the outcome: you don't shake hands with your executioner. In some situations, however, the mutual dependence is greater than others. The buyer of a Christmas present has considerable power in relation to a number of potential suppliers in being able to walk away from most of them without any personal disadvantage. The shop steward negotiating with the personnel manager cannot easily find another *management* with which to negotiate, even though he may find another *manager* to negotiate with ('Let me speak to the organ grinder instead of the monkey'). The research manager has one engineering manager only with whom to deal. When negotiators do not have a choice of adversary, negotiations are much more delicate, difficult and potentially fruitful.

Negotiation is likely to have a major, core issue. Influencing is a term used to cover a range of behaviours that are either more general or relatively minor. You influence someone to share your point of view, so that they too believe in the destruction of nuclear weapons, or that yours is the best golf club to join, or that it is high time the financial director got his come uppance. You influence people also by persuading them to pour you a second cup of tea, lend you money, or give you a job.

Negotiation and influencing share a number of aspects of approach and skill, although negotiation is usually more formal and representative, while influencing is more informal and personal.

Fundamental questions about preparing for negotiation

1 *Will it be negotiation or something else?*
Negotiation is appropriate only when there is a conflict of interest between parties, who need each other to find a mutually acceptable outcome from a particular problem. The main alternatives are forcing, when you impose terms on the other party to be accepted or rejected, and problem-solving when there is a common interest and mutual support.

2 *Will it be compromise or conjunction?*
Compromise is splitting the difference between the two parties. The seller wants £500, the buyer offers £400, and they agree on £450. This is seldom appropriate in more complex situations, as it is likely to satisfy neither party. Conjunction is exploring fully the conflicting interests of the parties and gradually putting together an agreement that provides the maximum benefits (and minimum costs) to both parties.

3 *Will the conflict be resolved or accommodated?*
When conflict is resolved, the adversaries become friends and exchange conflict of interests for common interest. Accommodation of conflict is when the interests of the parties remain different but they find a way of working together which is to their mutual satisfaction.

4 *Is the time right?*
For negotiation to be effective, both parties need a similar degree of interest in success. Partly this is a question of tension: are both parties under similar pressure to find a settlement? Partly it is a question of power: are the parties of roughly equal power in relation to each other regarding the negotiations that are to take place? The greater the imbalance of power between the parties, the more negative the attitudes of both. Parity of power is most likely to bring success.

The run-up to negotiations

1 Negotiators must know and agree their objectives.

2 There must be an agenda for the meeting that both parties understand and accept.

3 Each party should have one person to present their case and question the opposing case. Other members of the negotiating team may deal with specialist matters but should not obscure the main thrust the spokesman is developing. Team members who remain silent can be very helpful in discussions among team members during adjournments.

4 The setting for the meeting should make sure that the parties face each other, reflecting their divergent interests.

Influencing a group – the AIDA process

This is a way of structuring a presentation to a group of people that will persuade them to your point of view. It is based on a familiar sales training technique.

1 Compel the *Attention* of your listeners by quickly showing expertise, confidence and good intentions.

2 Awaken *Interest* in your audience by identifying needs they have which could be satisfied.

3 Create *Desire* for what you are offering by showing how it will satisfy their needs.

4 Ensure *Action* by making clear what they should do and linking the action you propose with the satisfaction of desire you have promised.

Stroking

Just as cats purr when stroked, so humans respond to being stroked, though the strokes are more likely to be words, smiles, frowns and nods.

Positive strokes are ways of saying 'you're O.K.' and make the recipient feel alert, confident and important.

Negative strokes are ways of saying 'you're not O.K.' and lead the recipient to feel hurt and inadequate.

Conditional strokes, both positive and negative, are standard ways of influencing the behaviour of other people. Positive conditional strokes (smiles, nods and agreement) may be given by a superior to a subordinate who is providing helpful advice; but these would change to negative conditional (frowns, yawns and irritability) when the subordinate produces bad advice.

Positive strokes are those most likely to produce a constructive response, as they strengthen the self confidence and responsiveness of the other person, but negative strokes are better than none, as they at least recognize the existence of the other person.

People who take the view 'I'm O.K.: you're O.K.' seek and offer mainly positive strokes.

People with the view 'I'm O.K.: you're not O.K.' offer mainly negative strokes.

People with the view 'I'm not O.K.: you're O.K.' seek negative strokes to confirm their comfortable (although helpless) feeling of dependency.

'I'm not O.K.: you're not O.K.' is a position of despair, with negative strokes offered and asked for.

Exercises

1 The last time you took part in negotiation, would it have been better for your party to have adopted a forcing or problem-solving mode? Could you have done so? How would the outcome have been different?

2 Pick out from today's newspaper an account of some situation of conflicting interests; diplomacy, war, industrial dispute or similar. Is the time right for negotiations? If not, how can greater power parity be achieved?

3 Make some rough notes, using the AIDA formula, for one of the following persuasions:

   a Getting your spouse and children to agree a change of venue for the summer holiday.

   b Getting a room in a hotel which is fully booked.

   c Persuading school leavers to join the Youth Training Scheme.

4 Spend a day at work reminding yourself, or persuading yourself, that you are O.K. and everyone else is O.K. Seek and offer only positive strokes. In the evening evaluate your experiences.

Further reading

MORLEY I E and STEPHENSON G M. *The Social Psychology of Bargaining*. London, Allen & Unwin, 1977

FISHER R and URY W. *Getting to Yes: Negotiating Agreement Without Giving in*. Cambridge, Mass., Harvard University Press, 1981

HARRIS T. *I'm O.K. – You're O.K.*. New York, Harper and Row, 1969

And finally . . .

Nearly 500 years ago a Florentine civil servant, Niccolò Machiavelli, produced a book, *The Prince*, to give rational advice to those in places of power. His counsel to the medieval prince is at least of interest to the twentieth century manager:

> A prince is to be respected when he is a true friend and a true enemy; when he declares himself on the side of one prince against another without any reservation . . . if you do not declare your intentions, you will always be the prey of the victor to the delight and satisfaction of the vanquished, and you will have no reason why anyone would come to your assistance; because whoever wins does not want reluctant allies who would not assist him in times of adversity; and whoever loses will not give you refuge since you were unwilling to run the risk of coming to his aid.
> Machiavelli N *The Prince*, Oxford, Oxford University Press, 1984, pp 74–5

8 Problem-solving

The effectiveness of many individual activities within organizations often depends on the quality of the ideas and the creativity produced and exercised in the solution of problems. The key to finding the answers to many of these problems lies principally in our ability to understand the nature of the problem in the first place.

It was one of G K Chesterton's characters who remarked that "it isn't that they can't see the solution, it is that they can't see the problem". A thorough analysis of the apparent problem via a process of decomposition and restructuring may lead to a redefinition of the problem. This process will often lead to the suggestion of additional solutions. For example, we may be trying to solve the apparent problem of whether to locate a new factory in Warrington or Motherwell, whereas the real problem is whether we need a new factory at all. In addition, there is a strong tendency to believe that the number of possible solutions is limited, but with most problems there is a large number of alternative solutions. Despite first appearances, there is rarely one solution which outclasses all the others. In any case, the first solution that springs to mind should not be chosen automatically without first generating and evaluating other possibilities. As the innovation expert Twiss, remarks, "it is rare for first thoughts to provide the most creative solution".

We can improve our problem-solving capacity personally by training ourselves to use a more creative approach. De Bono's now well known expression 'lateral thinking' (indicating the ability to escape from old ideas and generate new ones) requires us first to recognize the inflexibility of many of our current ways of thinking. Many dominant ideas in our minds can affect the way we approach problems in the first place: we make false assumptions, create unnecessary boundaries and reject compromises. Moreover, we are inclined to be single-minded, arrogant, impatient, partial or selective in our treatment of problems. However, de Bono believes that we have a potential advantage over more logical systems, since we can allow ourselves the luxury of being 'blurry-brained'; we can switch from one idea to the next and make abstractions which allow us to think. Computers, like most animals, are 'sharp-brained'; they are utterly trapped by existing ideas. People have the ability therefore to overcome these blocks to creative problem-solving.

There are also many group problem-solving techniques (see overleaf). Many of these rely on the production of creative ideas by means other than through the exercise of logical thought processes. Most of them use multi-disciplinary teams to bring together people from different intellectual backgrounds and with different mental constraints. The modern technologist or scientist, for example, is likely to be a convergent thinker (see Chapter 31). A multi-disciplinary team may be essential in order to achieve a combination of systematic analysis and imagination.

Managers can contribute also to the creative problem-solving abilities of the members of their departments by providing an environment which is receptive to unplanned creative ideas and where opportunities for the exercise of creativity are identified and encouraged.

The problem-solving process

1 *Define your problem*
Identify your objective: what ends are you trying to achieve? A need is a discrepancy between current and desired ends.

The objective must be as precise and measurable as possible (when, how much, etc), so that you will know whether or not you have been successful in your problem-solving exercise.

You may have to operate a trade off between competing objectives, for example keeping advertising expenditures stable and increasing sales.

2 *Redefine your problem*
A new definition of the problem may emerge as a result of decomposing and restructuring along the lines suggested above.

3 *Assess the solutions*
Select and consider alternative solutions (tools, methods, techniques or processes) to the problem in the light of the situation and weighed against the probable consequences.

4 *Select one solution*
Select and implement your chosen solution. This is invariably done when uncertainties still exist (see chapter 34).

5 *Evaluate*
Evaluate how well/badly your objectives have been met.

Components of the problem situation

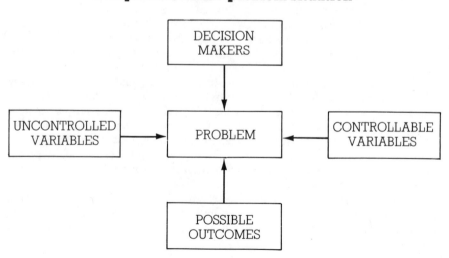

Group problem-solving techniques

SYNECTICS: Group discussion which seeks solutions in areas
                     other than that represented by the immediate
                     problem and which makes frequent use of
                     metaphors. Solutions are suggested which there-
                     fore may not otherwise be considered. For
                     example, when dealing with the problem of
                     managers with redundant skills, the problem is
                     redefined as being one of the need to recycle glass
                     bottles.

DIALECTICS: Different formulations of the problem by each
                     member of the group are judged critically against
                     each other, thus highlighting the effect which
                     different people's assumptions can have upon their
                     perceptions, even when the same data is used.

SEARCH CONFERENCE: A multi-disciplinary team pools its experiences,
                     values and knowledge in order to identify and
                     remove self-imposed constraints, and hence to
                     develop a shared perception of the problem.

BRAINSTORMING: The generation of a large number of unconven-
                     tional ideas by the suppression of tendencies to
                     criticize or to judge or reject prematurely (see
                     Chapter 31).

The nine-dot puzzle

The problem is to draw four straight lines to cover
all nine dots without lifting pencil from paper.
Most people will assume that they are restricted
by the shape formed by the dots – making it
virtually impossible to solve the puzzle. However,
if we reject this assumption, new courses of action
become possible. Try it!

Exercises

1 When faced with a problem, ask yourself:
     Do I really understand the problem involved?
     What am I trying to get done?
     Is this the best way to do it?
     What may go wrong when I put my solution into effect?

     (Dale & Michelon, op. cit., 1969)

   Make a conscious effort to use this problem-solving approach over the next few months.

2 Apply the problem-solving process detailed on the previous page to the question of buying a car.

Further reading

ACKOFF R L and VERGARA E. 'Creativity in Problem-solving and Planning: A Review, *European Journal of Operational Research*. Vol 7, No. 1, May 1981, pp 1–13

DALE E and MICHELON L C. *Modern Management Methods*, Harmondsworth, Middx., Penguin, 1969

DE BONO E. *Practical Thinking*. Harmondsworth, Middx., Penguin, 1976

RICKARD T. *Problem Solving Through Creative Analysis*, Epping, Essex, Gower, 1974

KAUFMAN R. *Identifying and Solving Problems: A System Approach*, La Jolla, Calif., University Associates, 1979

TWISS B C. *Managing Technological Innovation*, London, Longman, 1980

And finally . . .

In analyses of the value of group problem solving versus individual problem solving, groups produce better than the average individual's judgement, but are not as good as the most proficient individual. Groups tend to be more accurate but take longer than individuals in solving problems. In creativity exercises, individuals tend to 'dry up' before groups do.

9　Report-writing

Reports are written to be both read and acted upon. What the writer wants to say is not as important as what the reader wants to know and what the reader should do, so that reports are written not to interest nor even to inform, but to enable the reader to do something. This means that the action by the reader is the constant objective of the writer. Reports should be as brief as possible, but proposed action has to be thoroughly justified.

Before the writing begins there needs to be an outline, or *framework*. This will give a logical sequence to the writing and avoid risks of duplication, as well as presenting material early in the report that will be needed to justify points made later. The framework comes from analyzing the message that is to be sent in terms of the action expected and then subdividing the components of that message to be logically grouped. The framework may be modified until the writer is convinced that it is satisfactory.

The logical groups will be in *sections*, each dealing with a distinct aspect of the report material. This emphasizes the logic of the way the material is grouped, but it is a part also of the communication to the reader, because the sections have titles, like headlines in a newspaper, which sum up what the section contains. Titles should not tease or muddle the reader. 'Which way now?' for example is an unhelpful title as it poses a question without giving any clue of the answer.

The *paragraph* is a unit of thought in the writing, dealing with a single topic or idea, and good paragraphing will ensure the material is read:

> Paragraphing is a matter of the eye. A reader will address himself more readily to his task if he sees from the start that he will have breathing spaces from time to time than if what is before him looks like a marathon course
>
> Fowler, 1968, p. 435

The appropriate length of paragraph varies with the material being written. Textbooks usually average 100–20 words, popular novels 60–75 and popular newspapers 30–40. Short paragraphs are easier for the reader, but reports will sometimes require detailed argument involving greater length. It is wise to keep the average under 100, if possible.

The *sentence* is the bit of writing between full stops, which makes sense and usually has a subject and a finite verb. The main difficulty in writing sentences is either that they are too long or that they set up expectations that are not realized. Too long sentences come about through adding on extra clauses and qualifications.

Setting up expectations that are not realized come from inferring what is to come in the sentence, but then moving on to a qualifying clause without returning to the original thought.

Report writer's checklist

1 *Before writing*
   a What action do you expect from this report?
   b Who will read it?
   c How short can it be?

2 *Outline*
   a What precisely is the topic of the report?
   b How many components are there?
   c How can those best be grouped?
   d How are the components brought into sections?
   e Do the titles inform the reader?
   f Will the report, as outlined, produce the action specified in 1a?

3 *Writing the report*
   a Is the average paragraph length less than 100 words?
   b Have you used more words than are needed?
   c Have you used words that are precise and concrete rather than words that are vague and abstract?
   d Have you any superfluous adverbs, adjectives and roundabout phrases?
   e Have you shown the source of any facts quoted?
   f Are any of the sentences too long?

4 *Revising the report*
   a Will the report, as written, produce the action specified in 1a?
   b Is anything missing?
   c Are any calculations accurate?
   d Are the recommendations clear and justified?
   e Is the choice between alternatives clear?
   f Is any part of the report likely to cause offence to anyone? If so, can that be avoided?
   g What objections do you expect to the recommendations, and how will you deal with them?
   h Can any of the possible objections be prevented by rewriting part of the report?

5 *Final presentation*
   a Is the typing perfect and without spelling mistakes?
   b Are all the pages numbered?
   c Are abbreviations and symbols used consistently throughout?
   d Does the general appearance of the report encourage the reader to read it?
   e Is there a single page summary of proposals?
   f Is the report being distributed to all the appropriate people?
   g If the report is confidential, is that indicated on the report and ensured by the method of distribution?

Some problems in writing

1 *Active and passive voice* The active voice is more direct and vigorous than the passive, so 'the roof leaks when it rains' is better than 'leaking is caused when the roof is rained on'.

2 *Cant* describes meaningless phrases that have become meaningless through repetition, like 'by and large'. These are also known as clichés.

3 *Jargon* is vocabulary specialized to a trade, profession or other group. It is useful shorthand for those who know, but bewildering to those who do not.

4 *Non sequitur* This is where the conclusion does not follow from the evidence, like the argument that computers will revolutionize management practice because they could.

5 *Syllepsis* is where metaphor is linked to the literal to make nonsense: 'She sat with her head in her hands and her eyes on the floor'.

6 *Tautology* is repeating what has already been said whilst implying extra meaning. 'Behaviour pattern' says no more than 'behaviour'; in the phrase '... not limited only to ...' there is no need for 'only'.

Punctuation

Comma makes a logical division within a sentence:
a to separate the subject from descriptive words or phrases, 'Charles, Prince of Wales, plays polo.'
b to separate clauses, 'if he scores, the crowd will cheer.'
c to separate items on a list, 'his parents, wife and children came to watch.'

Semi colon links two sentences so closely related that a full stop would make too great a break, 'he didn't score; Jones did.'

Colon separates an announcement from what is announced, 'the order of play is as follows:'

Apostrophe indicates either a possessive, 'the team's performance' or a missing syllable in abbreviations, 'it's time for tea.'

Clichés to avoid

Afford an opportunity
Arguably
As it were
At the end of the day
At the present time
At this point in time
Be that as it may
For that matter
For the purpose of
Generally speaking
Give rise to
In a manner of speaking
In such a manner as to
In respect of
In the near future
In point of fact
Much of a muchness
No way
Owing to the fact that
Without fear or favour
Without fear of contradiction
With regard to

Exercises

1 Reduce the second paragraph at the beginning of this chapter to improve its impact at the same time as reducing the number of words.

2 Review a report you have written using the points in section four of the report writer's checklist. How many alterations to the structure would you make?

3 Refer back to the first chapter of this book. Approximately what proportion of the sentences on a single page could be made shorter without losing any meaning?

4 When do you use a hyphen, brackets, inverted commas and an exclamation mark?

Further reading

ADAIR J. *Training for Communication*. Aldershot, Hants., Gower, 1978
FOWLER H W. *Modern English Usage*. 2nd edition, Oxford, Oxford University Press, 1968
MAYERSON E W. *Shoptalk*. Philadelphia, Pa., Saunders, 1979
The Oxford Dictionary for Writers and Editors. Oxford, Clarendon Press, 1981

And finally . . .

It is always possible to trim out what is not necessary, as suggested in these last few pages, but there remains the need for some *style* to the writing. The reader needs not only accurate writing, but also a rhythm in the writing that makes it comfortable to read. Sometimes the bare, plain facts do not speak for themselves and the reader has to be persuaded to a point of view.

10 Reading

Many managers grumble about the amount of reading involved in their jobs. It is one of the duties that many feel impedes their progress in getting on with the 'real' work. This does not mean that all managers need to be able to read everything more quickly, but they need to be able to read effectively. The first step is to distinguish the types of reading that are involved.

First is reading for identification. Is the material to be thrown away as unimportant, filed against a possible future need, passed on to someone else, or kept to be read by the recipient? The reader will be looking mainly for the source and topic of the material to make this judgement. Second is reading for information, where the reader will be looking for the message in the writing: the request being made, the cost of the proposal, the date of the meeting or whatever specific piece of information is sought. This requirement produces the interest in reports that have the summary of proposals on a single sheet of paper. Sometimes the material will then be passed on to someone else, sometimes it will be kept for more careful study and sometimes it will be thrown away.

Reading for identification and reading for information are activities where speed and selectivity of the reader are valuable attributes. The next type is reading for understanding, where speed can be a hindrance. Now the reader is looking not for the message or 'the bottom line' but the reasoning that has led to the proposals and the evidence that is presented to support the argument. An example would be a tender for building work to be carried out. The reader would look first for identification and information: the source of the tender and its price. In then moving on to understand it, a check would be made of what was included and what excluded, what materials were to be used, how long the work was to take, how payment was required and so forth. Sometimes this process takes on aspects of creative imagination where the reader looks for inferences. Readers of job references, for instance, frequently believe that they can discern hidden messages that are written between the lines, and those assessing competing business tenders look for indications of enthusiasm and determination among those submitting tenders.

A fourth type of reading is for criticism: looking for weaknesses or inconsistencies in what is written. This requires very detailed and careful examination of what is presented, with possible flaws mulled over and probably discussed with colleagues. This is found sometimes in the review of submitted tenders, so that queries can be put to the potential supplier with a view to re-submission. It is found in the drafting and negotiating of agreements and in proposals for commercial amalgamations.

Although it is generally true that most managers could read more quickly without losing effectiveness at any level, quicker reading could be an advantage to those reading for identification and information while being a handicap to those reading for understanding or criticism.

Drill for reading for identification

1 Who is it from?
2 Who (else) is it to?
3 What is it about?
4 How important is it?

Alernative actions

⎰
1 Throw away
2 File
3 Pass to ......
4 Read
⎱

Drill for reading for information

1 Scan a full page at a time with a general left-right movement of the eyes, but 'pushing' down the centre of the page.

2 Use the opening of paragraphs as clues to significant information being imminent.

3 Pick out headings, illustrations, italics, underlinings, lists.

4 Check pages to scan by checking contents list and index for clues to content.

5 Look for phrases that signal conclusions and summary statements:

'Therefore I believe . . .'
'The outcome of this is . . .'
'In contrast to this . . .'
'We suggest . . .'
'In conclusion . . .'

Preparing to read for understanding

1 Decide how much you are going to read at a session and stop when you have done it. This will assist both your understanding and your recall by giving you the satisfaction of fulfilling the contract you have made with yourself. When reading for understanding it can be unhelpful to read up to an immovable deadline, such as when your train reaches its destination, as you may be obliged to stop just before the penny drops.

2 Review what you already know about the subject. Either run the thoughts through your mind, check notes you have made previously or get a quick briefing from a colleague. If the material is completely new, it may be helpful to check in a reference book, like looking up salient facts about the economy of a country before reading a market research report on prospects for doing business there. This provides a framework for the reading.

3 Read with a purpose. Decide why you are reading the material and set yourself a short list of questions that you want answered.

Reading for understanding

1 Make notes: this makes your reading active, as you have to decide what to note and what not to note. The easiest way of doing this is with a pencil to underline phrases, make marks in the margin and scribble queries. A development of this is to use a text highlighter, which paints a coloured, transparent layer over your selected passage. However, this should be used very selectively, in order not to defeat the object of the exercise. If you write out notes on a separate sheet of paper, you are developing both understanding and recall as you are giving yourself the task both of deciding what material to select and then summarizing it in your own words.

   Taking a photocopy is no substitute for understanding.

2 Review your notes. See if the marginal queries you pencilled in the first time have been resolved by your later reading. Have you missed an important feature that you did not appreciate until your first reading was complete? If there is anything you still do not understand, how can you resolve it? Do your notes make sense? Are there gaps?

Reading for criticism

1 What does not make sense?

2 What conclusions are not convincingly supported by argument and facts?

3 Where is evidence used to produce a conclusion when a different conclusion is equally, or more, feasible?

4 Are any facts incorrect or out of date?

Tips for reading more quickly

1 Avoid vocalizing, ie silently speaking the words as they are read. This reduces reading speed to speaking speed; speed will increase if the habit can be broken. Keep the lips shut tight and concentrate on not sounding the words.

2 Reduce the number of fixations, which is the number of time the eyes stop when scanning a line of type. Practise fixing on two words at a time, then three words and four words.

3 Use a cursor, which is a finger, a pencil or a piece of card, that you move along the line of type and down the page in front of the eyes. It focusses the eyes and leads them to move more quickly and more smoothly. This method is invariably used by people adding a column of figures but seldom used for the equally useful purpose of increasing reading speed.

Exercises

1 Using a pencil as a cursor, read the first page of the next chapter, taking a note of the time it takes you. Do that before reading any further on this page.

How long did it take? If it took more than two minutes, you could certainly increase your speed.

How many characteristics of Type A managers can you recall?

How many of Smith's six major sources of stress can you recall? If you recall fewer than four in answer to the first question and fewer than five in answer to the second, your comprehension is below average. If this is associated with a reading speed of less than 90 seconds, you are probably reading too fast.

2. Re-read the opening chapter using the suggestions on the previous page regarding reading for understanding. In the same way, read two consecutive pages of your daily newspaper for information, followed by a leader for criticism.

Further reading

BUZAN T. *How to Make the Most of Your Mind*, London, Colt Books, 1977, Chapter 5

DE LEEUW M and E. *Read Better, Read Faster*, Harmondsworth, Middx., Penguin Books, 1965

And finally . . .

Reading maketh a full man; conference a ready man; and writing an exact man.

Francis Bacon 1561–1626

Reading is to the mind what exercise is to the body.

Richard Steele 1672–1729

Education has produced a vast population able to read but unable to distinguish what is worth reading.

G M Trevelyan 1876–1961

11 Coping with stress

Managers often complain of having stressful jobs or stressful days at work. To be stressed has become almost a badge of status and importance in some circles.

What do we mean by stress? Stress is a demand made on our physical or mental energy. Where this is felt as excessive it is experienced as stressful and may lead to stress related physiological symptoms. The first symptoms may be irritability, excessive drinking, depression, raised blood pressure, headaches and chest pains. These can lead ultimately to diseases such as ulcers, coronary heart disease and mental illness. This definition implies that people will experience stress in different circumstances and some are able to cope better than others. One distinction that has been made is between type A people and type B. Type A are coronary prone and characterized by excessive competitiveness, alertness, irritability, feelings of responsibility and completely involved with their work. Type B are calmer characters, at less risk of suffering coronary heart disease. Although the clinical evidence for this distinction is being debated, we can all recognize ourselves and those we work with as tending towards type A or B. The useful point is that what is stressful to one person may not be to another, because we have different personalities, expertize and abilities.

Smith et al (1982) identify six major sources of stress. First, every job has some aspects where someone, sometime will find a source of stress. There can be too much to do, too little, or the work may be too difficult. Secondly, managers may be uncertain about what to do, or they may have conflicting demands made upon them. Where the job involves responsibility for people this uncertainty is likely to increase and consequently lead to more stress. Thirdly, the nature of relations at work can be stressful, particularly where there is mistrust. Fourthly, managers may experience stress because of their career prospects. This can be either through lack of job security or feeling that their status is unsuitable; both under-promotion and over-promotion can be sources of pressure. Fifthly, the organizational climate can inhibit an individual's freedom and personal control. The more participation is permitted the less stress is felt. Sixthly, a suitable balance between work and life outside the organization can be difficult to achieve. Pressure can come from the conflict of demands or crises. How to distribute time and commitment between home and work without the problems from one overflowing and creating problems in the other can become stressful.

These sources of stress are problems for the individual manager. They are also a problem for the organization as a whole if individuals are unable to work effectively. Poor quality and quantity of work creates problems for others in the organization. So managers need to cope with their own stress and with potential sources of stress in others. Whether this adds to the sources of stress for the managers themselves is an open question!

Dealing with the sources of stress

1 *In the job*
   Short term stress can be stimulating. Try to get it out of the way as soon as possible. Decide your priorities and stick to them.
   Long term stress What are you doing that could be done by someone else? Are you treating everything with equal importance? Is this appropriate? Have you acquired new responsibilities without discarding some of the previous ones? Are you still doing your old job? What about discussing your job description with your boss or colleagues?

2 *Uncertainty and conflicting demands*
   Ask for clarification from the boss. Try the assertiveness techniques described in chapter 6. The job is yours and you probably have more control over it than you think. Start by thinking about the choices open to you as described in chapter 3. Set down your own goals using goal planning, as in chapter 33.

3 *Poor working relationship with a colleague*
   If the difficulty is caused because the two of you have different goals, try to appreciate the other point of view and see if you can do some mutual goal-setting. Alternatively, the problem may be caused by misunderstanding that you need to root out.

4 *Career prospects*
   The management ethic includes the idea of always going 'up', so that you may be classed as a failure if you are not seeking and gaining promotion. But what life style suits you best? In any hierarchy there are more middle managers than senior managers, so do you want to gain your satisfaction from doing well the job you have rather than looking for another? More seniority seldom makes a person more secure in their job.

5 *Organizational climate*
   Is the climate as prohibitive as you think? Or is it an excellent excuse? What happens if you do try? Can you change it? Would another organization be any better?

Stability zones

We can cope with a lot of change, pressure, complexity and confusion if at least one area of our lives is relatively stable. Toffler (1970) suggested these stability zones were all important. The main kinds of stability zones are: ideas, places, people and organizations. We all need at least one of these secure. Working out where your stability zones are and maintaining them helps to cope with stress in other areas.

Relaxation

Sit or lie down comfortably, close your eyes and concentrate on relaxing.

Starting at the top of your head feel each part of your body relax and get heavier.

When the head feels heavy concentrate on the eyelids, mouth, chin, left hand, arm and so on down the body.

Breathe through your nose and listen to your own breathing. It will get slower and slower.

Try doing this every day starting with ten minutes and working up to 20 minutes.

There are various techniques and courses run on relaxation. Yoga and meditation are well known. Bio-feedback techniques tell you when the pulse rate or breathing are reduced. Tapes that instruct one to relax might be worth a try.

Various other strategies

Exercise Physical exercise uses the adrenalin that stress produces in the body.
Change of scene A weekend away or a holiday can distract from the sources of stress. Cynics maintain this is the main purpose of training courses!
Life-planning What do you want out of life? At home, at work, in your free time?
Therapy and self help groups Any group that listens and treats us seriously as individuals will provide a stability zone to help us cope with stress.
The spouse or close friends Invaluable for listening and putting things into perspective.

Exercises

1 Justify to your employing organization why they should pay for you to go on a skiing holiday rather than a week's management training course costing the same.

2 What are your stability zones? What have you done to cultivate and maintain them this week?

Further reading

PEDLER M, BURGOYNE J and BOYDELL T. *A Manager's Guide to Self Development*. Maidenhead, Berks., McGraw-Hill, 1978

SMITH M, BECK J, COOPER C L COX C, OTTAWAY D and TALBOT R. *Introducing Organisational Behaviour*. London, MacMillan, 1982

STEWART R. *Choices for Managers*. Maidenhead, Berks., McGraw-Hill, 1982

TOFFLER A. *Future Shock*. London, Pan, 1970

And finally . . .

However stressed a manager may feel it is a sobering thought that those lower in the hierarchy show more symptoms of stress than those higher up the ladder.

It's a relief when you get off the moving line. It's such a tremendous relief. I can't put it into words. When your on the line it's on top of you all the time. You may feel ill, not one hundred per cent but the line will be one hundred per cent.

H. Beynon *Working for Ford*, Harmondsworth, Middx., Penguin, 1973 p. 118

B   Working in the Organization

Having organized oneself and established a style of working with other people, there is then a series of issues that have to be understood about working in an organizational context.

First is the need to understand the ways in which organizational structures vary and the significance of political behaviour within those frameworks. Six of the chapters in this section deal with how the manager analyzes the general organizational situation and then works out strategies for survival and effectiveness in that corporate jungle. There are a number of links back to parts of the first section of the book, especially in the analysis of one's network of contacts and the chapter on organizational communication, which develops the suggestions made in chapter 5.

This is followed by two chapters on aspects of working in small groups and the roles of group members, after which there is a consideration of the very specialized activity that is involved when people work in committees. The concluding chapter on dealing with change examines the nature of change and the problems it poses for managers, and then moves on to consider how the individual manager can best implement changes that are necessary in a way that will invoke collaboration with the initiative rather than resistance to it.

Whether they have many subordinates or none, all managers have to cope with life in an organization. Being successful requires not only professional competence and sound personal organization, it requires the ability to understand the processes of organization and to use the strength and potential that the organization provides for collaborative action and constructive competition. The message of this part of the book can be summed up in two quotations from Edmund Burke:

"Good order is the foundation of all things . . ."

but also:

"A state without the means of some change is without the means of its conservation."

12 Forms of organization

Organization is the start of the process that makes people together achieve what they cannot do individually. It is the distribution of power to make decisions and get things done, choosing which skills and expertize to group together, and deciding how working groups interconnect and communicate. Because organization limits individual freedom of action, people will often fight against it, trying to 'short circuit the system' or 'cut through the red tape'. The harder you work at getting the organization right for your situation, the less will be the fighting against it; but it must be appropriate to your business and the people who are involved. Overleaf we describe four types of organizational structure. Although seldom found in pure form, they represent features that will be found in most businesses.

Organizing begins with labelling. Every organization member has a label explaining the content and boundaries of her or his job. The employee needs the label to answer questions like 'What do you want me to do?' 'How much scope have I got?' 'Where does my job fit in with everyone else's?' and (perhaps) 'How and when can I get promoted?' There are also questions about other people's labels, 'Who do I ask about . . . ?' 'Who is in charge?' 'Who else do I work with?' Without good labelling there is uncertainty and inefficiency. Often the label is no more than a job title, which is enough when it is explicit and widely understood, like electrician or cook, but vague titles usually require a job description to make clear the duties and, especially, the boundaries of jobs.

The second step is grouping, deciding the membership of various working groups and how their activities interconnect. What skills and functions should be grouped together into different departments and divisions? What grouping will lead to effective collaboration rather than dissatisfaction and attempts to beat the system?

The scope of decisions to be made by individuals will be defined by their labels or by their positions in the groupings, but some decisions are made collectively by decision-making complexes (DMCs). These may be committees, councils, teams or groups.

The fourth feature is operating procedures: the ways in which decisions are implemented, and the standard ways of getting things done in the organization. How are purchase orders authorized? When new employees join the company, how are they included on the payroll?

All of these can lead to inefficiency and frustration when they go wrong and they are then difficult to put right. The usual method is 're-organization' which involves changing labels and groupings, often in a panic and seldom including attention to DMCs and procedures. These moves may have more to do with assertions of power and problems of status than with problems of organization. Balancing the power and influence of personalities is important, but it is not a sufficient principle on which to base all organizational decisions.

The *Entrepreneurial* form emphasizes power at the centre. One person or small group is so dominant that all power stems from there, all decisions are made in the light of central expectations and all people in the organization mirror central behaviour. This sort of strong centralization is found often where there is a need to move fast and to take major decisions needing flair and judgement rather than a measured weighing of alternatives.

Few decisions are taken collectively, there is little dependence on procedures, and actions stem from getting the approval of key figures, with decisions often based on precedent. This form is how most organizations begin life, with the logic of depending on the special knowledge of the founder who made the business possible. In large, functional undertakings it is usually found in areas like marketing, among people who enjoy individual power, risk and competition.

The *Bureaucratic* form groups jobs by some common feature, like function or location, and groups them in a hierarchy of responsibility to distribute power among members of the organization. Emphasis is on role rather than flair and judgement. In stable situations bureaucracy makes possible economies of scale and the benefits of job specialization. It is seldom flexible enough to be suitable for volatile situations.

Action stems from consistent use of procedures, often incorporating decision-making by committee to ensure thorough consideration of issues and to guard against corruption. This form tends to be liked by those seeking clearly-defined duties and responsibilities.

The *Matrix* form has been developed to overcome some of the shortcomings of the first two. A conventional hierarchy has a second set of hierarchical connections laid over the first, and running at right angles to it. The vertical lines are of function, but the horizontal lines link people from different functions to share full responsibility for a particular project requiring skills from each function, making each member a functional plenipotentiary for the duration of the project.

Action is based on expertize in a specific context and it can be a popular form for those wanting not only to deploy their skills but also to enjoy a sense of responsibility and contribution. Although first used to cope with the complex organizational demands of high technology, it has lost favour because it tends to cause costly support services and unwieldly administration.

The *Independence* form is a type of non-organization. Instead of putting the contributions of people together so that the sum is greater than the parts, the organization is no more than a support system enabling individuals to perform.

Many professional practices and consultants work in this way, so that barristers' chambers and doctors' clinics provide the facilities for them to work separately rather than together. The form is attractive to those who are independently-minded and confident of their ability to be individually successful. Although it has been regarded as unsuitable for most types of job, the growing number of free-lance specialists and others working from home has increased interest in this form.

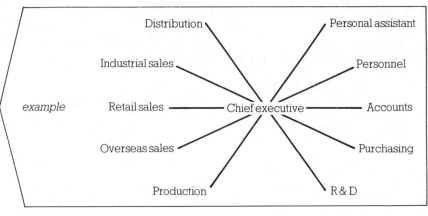

example

- Distribution
- Industrial sales
- Retail sales ——— Chief executive
- Overseas sales
- Production
- Personal assistant
- Personnel
- Accounts
- Purchasing
- R & D

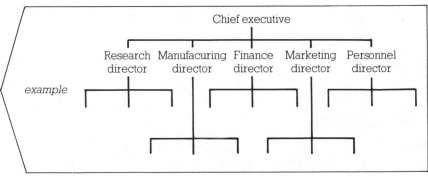

example

Chief executive

Research director | Manufacuring director | Finance director | Marketing director | Personnel director

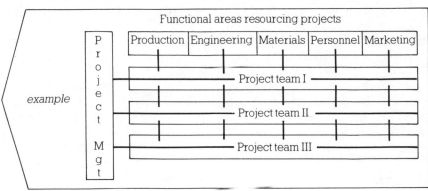

example

Functional areas resourcing projects

Project Mgt

| Production | Engineering | Materials | Personnel | Marketing |

Project team I

Project team II

Project team III

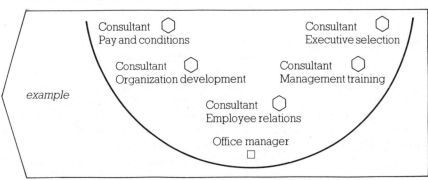

example

- Consultant ⬡ Pay and conditions
- Consultant ⬡ Executive selection
- Consultant ⬡ Organization development
- Consultant ⬡ Management training
- Consultant ⬡ Employee relations
- Office manager ▢

Exercises

1 For the organizational situations listed below, which of the four forms of organization would you regard as most suitable?

 a The flight deck of a passenger aircraft
 b Developing sophisticated weaponry to military specifications
 c The high street branch of a retail bank
 d A sales force
 e A school
 f An orchestra

2 How would you describe the emphasis in the organization of your present company?

3 Think of some jobs in your organization and decide how a change of label for them might improve efficiency.

4 In your organization, which DMCs should be replaced by individual decision makers and which decisions made by individuals would be better taken by DMCs?

Further reading

CHILD J. *Organization*. 2nd ed, London, Harper and Row, 1984

HANDY C B. *Understanding Organizations*. 3rd ed, Harmondsworth, Middx., Penguin, 1985

PETERS T J and WATERMAN R H. *In Search of Excellence*. London, Harper and Row, 1982

LEAVITT H J, DILL W R and EYRING H B. *The Organizational World*. New York, Harcourt, Brace, Jovanovich, 1973

The very readable book by Charles Handy has been popular since the first edition appeared in 1976, due to its imagination and realism. Child's book is more academic, but both of these authors write mainly for a British audience. *In Search of Excellence* has been a publishing phenomenon in the United States, selling over one million copies. The fourth text, *The Organizational World*, which was adopted by the Open University, is attractively written and full of practical suggestions.

And finally . . .

Peters and Waterman, mentioned above, point out the risk of regarding reorganizing as being all the required answer to cope with change:

> **. . . an organization chart is not a company, nor a new strategy an automatic answer to corporate grief. We all know this; but like as not, when trouble lurks, we call for a new strategy and probably re-organize. And when we re-organize, we usually stop at re-arranging the boxes on the chart. The odds are high that nothing much will change.**
>
> **PETERS T J and WATERMAN R H. *In Search of Excellence, op cit*, p. 3**

13 Organizational Politics

Power is an inescapable part of management. One of the main purposes of organizational charts is to describe the formal allocation of power to job titles. Organizational politics is the use of power in organizations. It involves any activity that seeks to acquire, develop and use power and other resources to ensure a particular outcome where various options are possible.

If there were always total agreement about objectives and how to achieve them there would be no need to change or influence another. The very nature of organizations, with their variety of individuals, groups and interests, inevitably lead to conflict. There is conflict over the priority of objectives and the use of resources. So power is an important attribute and the use of that power is political action. Many meetings within organizations are convened with the main purpose of resolving the conflict between two groups, for example the relative responsibilities of the day and night shift; maintenance and production schedules; the use of the conference room.

Managers frequently reject the idea of behaving politically as the word carries connotations of insincerity and deviousness. It may well be that it often involves these behaviours, but those who understand and use power are more able to get things done. As Dahl says:

> 'the graveyards of history are strewn with the corpses of reformers who failed utterly to reform anything, of revolutionaries who failed to win power . . . of anti-revolutionaries who failed to prevent a revolution – men and women who failed not only because of the forces arrayed against them but because the pictures in their minds about power and influence were simplistic and inaccurate.'
>
> Dahl, *op cit*, p. 15

The difficulty, almost inevitably for managers, is getting the balance right. We have been describing political behaviours and yet many management development programmes advocate openness, which it is hoped will result in relationships with colleagues becoming candid and constructive with the integrity of each being respected. Neither politics nor openness is the total solution, but both are necessary and they need not be incompatible. Extremes of 'politicking' are destructive and undesirable. Openness can guard against such extremes. For an organization to work at all there has to be a distribution of power within the structure to get things done, yet that very distribution is divisive and produces stresses on the structure and members of the organization. It is when that stress becomes too great that effectiveness declines. One way to assess whether one's own political behaviour is acceptable or not is to ask 'Why am I seeking this power?' 'What am I going to use it for?' If the answer is 'to meet some objective agreed with others', the result is likely to be an increase in organizational effectiveness, but if the answer is 'to get one over on the other person' then organizational effectiveness will probably be impaired.

Chapter 25, which deals with power and authority, is closely allied to the material of this chapter.

Techniques used to obtain power[1]

Technique	Benefit to self and organization	Drawback for self and organization
Alliances Collaborate with others where interests are sufficiently similar	Have someone on your side; their resources and skills.	Degree of commitment; not easy to discard, as a discarded ally becomes an enemy
Lobby Get support from others on particular issues		
Doing favours Provide services, support, information, materials and expect reciprocation		If done too much, others become suspicious
Being present at meeting or conference where important decision is taken	Interest is heard; you are involved in decision-making	Time consuming
Cornering resources Gathering people and materials into one's own area	Number of staff and size of budget can be measured, unlike most management activities	Empire-building is not necessarily related to to organization's objective
Being indispensible Either through expertise or by being an essential part of the administrative process	Can become an authority	Can become obsolete
Reciprocal support for patron Having a 'god-father' in a powerful position	Better to be pulled up the hierarchy than to push oneself up	Patron likely to exact fealty
Being able to cope with uncertainty Those who have expertize to deal with crises such as mending the machine or seeing a way round the problem		Only powerful in a crises, so crises may be created.

[1] Sources of power are discussed in chapter 25.

The importance of organizational politics to the manager

1 It helps to influence what and how something is done.

2 Members of organizations have to compete with each other for resources and to develop their careers.

3 As management performance is difficult to measure, building areas of influence is an alternative way of showing one's ability.

4 There is an increase in political activity when decisions are taken by committees, task groups and alliances, rather than by individual managers.

5 Favourable job mobility within an organization requires political awareness.

6 Organizations operate in a political context, due to international events, government policies and the activities of competitors.

Getting the balance right

The key to getting an effective level of political activity is to remember the distinction between networks and agendas described in chapter 2.

If managers have too much network and too little agenda they will be more concerned with being managers than with getting on with the job. If they are over-concerned with agendas and they under-emphasize networks, they may be too inward-looking and not get their agendas implemented.

Exercises

1 Which techniques for gaining power have you used? Which have you found effective?

2 Make a list of the various parts of your job. Which of these has a political slant? Which would you consider to be non-political? Which do you spend time worrying over?

3 What would you consider to be politicking in others?

Further reading

DAHL J. *Modern Political Analysis*. 2nd ed, London, Prentice Hall, 1970
JAY A. *Management and Machiavelli*. Harmondsworth, Middx., Penguin, 1967
MACHIAVELLI N. *The Prince*. Harmondsworth, Middx., Penguin, 1981
PFEFFER J. *Power in Organizations*. London, Pitman, 1981

And finally . . .

Some definitions:

Power **is the ability to influence other people to do something they would not otherwise do.**

Authority **is to have legitimate power, either through position or expertize.**

Politics **is the way in which power is put into action.**

Organizational politics **are ways of gaining and using power in an organization to get preferred results.**

Politicking **is seeking and using power for its own sake rather than to achieve agreed objectives.**

14 Knowing your own organizational system

It is important to know the system we work in. If we understand the system it is easier to use it effectively to get things done. The who, how, what, when and why also become clearer. Included in this chapter are both the organization's formal written systems and the informal, house style, that has evolved.

If we know the system it is clearer *who* to influence to get desired decisions, who has the information, who has the authority to sign, whose support one needs. To know *how* to do things will enable us to distinguish those that prefer informal phone calls from those whose telex requests are copied to all who can bring political pressure. Systems can vary in *what* an individual manager is expected to do. Some expect a lot of consultation with those above, alongside and below in the hierarchy. Others expect managers to be autonomous. The nature of the task will determine *when* things are done but so will the system. A role culture normally has a longer time scale than a club culture (*see* chapter 2). *Why* things are done also produces different answers. Organizations have different orientations to the market, time, people and formality.

One aspect of organizational life to look at when trying to understand the system is to try to find out what integrating techniques are used. These are necessary to manage the potential sources of conflict in organizations. For example, the conflict of a sales crisis and inflexible production schedule; the introduction of new technology and training programmes; the work of individuals in a department. Organizational structures vary with both flat and steep hierarchies. They have crossover points built in as integrators. The organization chart indicates how the work of separate units is integrated by reporting to a senior manager, so that if a conflict cannot be resolved it is passed up the hierarchy for a decision. Rule books and procedures define the responsibility of the units and individuals. By standardizing work and outlining the autonomy of jobs these techniques seek to anticipate conflicts by allocating responsibility to particular individuals. If an appeal to the rules does not provide a satisfactory answer, one of the other integrating devices has to be used. But procedures allow units and individuals to carry on working without constant reference up the hierarchy (see chapter 26). Planning devices is another technique used to indicate how the work of all is coordinated. Corporate plans show the contribution expected from units. These in turn are divided into specific objectives for departments and to objectives for individual managers. Budgets are similarly used to control and integrate individual contributions. Getting people together for discussions, in meetings, committees or task forces are increasingly formal ways organizations integrate the activities of members. Coordinators, whether individuals, departments or teams, are also used. These need to have a high level of expertize, as well as position in the hierarchy, so that all accept their resolutions.

Sources of information about your organizational system

	FORMAL	INFORMAL
WHO	Organization charts say who has the power and authority Hierarchy says who reports to whom	Your network (see chapter 16) Gossip will tell who has the information, influence, ideas
HOW	Rules say how to behave Procedures state how things should be done	Training will include the house style of 'how we do it' Custom and practice gleaned from colleagues
WHAT	Job descriptions say what the job involves Plans say what is intended Budgets state what money has been allocated	Chat with colleagues establishes who does what Discussions with people whose jobs might overlap establishes who will do what
WHEN	Contract dates say when delivery is due Action items from meetings say when it will be done Schedules show when to do things so all is coordinated	Groups establish routines
WHY	Contract of employment states the conditions of employment	Political network might give additional reasons to the formal systems

The pay off for improving your knowledge of your organizational system

1 To get resources such as information, materials and people, as effectively as possible

2 To know where the bottle necks are and how to avoid them

3 To influence the system towards your preferred outcome

4 To see if any changes are necessary

5 To understand the power distribution and so know who can affect things

---

The four types of organizational system (according to Handy)

Adaptive How the organization copes with the economic, social and physical environment; how it reaches decisions about the future; how policies are made.

Operating Systems to deal with the daily input, treatment and output eg production, sales, finance, purchasing. They deal with the daily running of the organization.

Maintenance These keep the organization effective. There are systems to reward and control personnel. How effort from diffferent units is coordinated.

Information This type of system serves the above three by providing the basis for monitoring, making decisions and taking action.

How to distinguish an organization from a mob

According to Argyris and Schön, when a mob begins to meet three conditions it becomes an organization. It must devise procedures for:

1 making decisions in the name of the collectivity;

2 delegating to individuals the authority to act for the collectivity;

3 setting boundaries between the collectivity and the rest of the world.

Consequently, employees will use the pronoun "we" when referring to their organization, thereby enabling organizational decisions and action to be taken.

Exercises

1 See if you can add to the table on sources of information about organizational systems. These can be general or specific to your organization.

2 When conflict arises in your organization how is it resolved?

    a appeals to the hierarchy?

    b looking at written prescriptions such as the rule book, procedures or job description?

    c looking at medium and long term plans, objectives and budgets?

    d getting people together formally or informally?

    e seeking expert advice?

3 Using Handy's types, how does your employing organization deal with the first three types of system? What information systems are used? How effectively do they meet the needs of the first three systems?

Further reading

ARGYRIS C and SCHÖN D. *Organizational Learning*. Reading, Mass., Addison Wesley, 1978

CHILD J. *Organization*. 2nd ed, London, Harper and Row, 1984

HANDY C. *Understanding Organizations*. 3rd ed, Harmondsworth, Middx., Penguin, 1985

LAWRENCE P and LORSCH J. *Organization and Environment*. Cambridge, Mass., Harvard University Press, 1967

MINTZBERG H. *Structure in Fives: designing effective organizations*. Englewood Cliffs, N.J., Prentice Hall, 1983

KHANDWHALLA P N. *Design of Organizations*. New York, Harcourt, Brace, Jovanovich, 1977

And finally . . .

Knowing the system helps the effective manager: but knowing only the system makes a manager very vulnerable. As those who have spent their careers in one organization find, if they leave, their skills in using that particular system are not necessarily transferable. All systems are not the same.

15 Dealing with problems of organization

Organizations may be over-managed through having too many people whose job is to coordinate and integrate the work of others. Well- meaning delegation can produce small packets of responsibility that slow down action because of the large number of people to be consulted and informed. This is especially a problem for those who see themselves as 'managed' rather than 'managing', because they see management as a confused collection of people, few of whom appear able to provide a clear decision or authoritative guidance. It is also a problem for senior managers, who feel distanced from the people engaged on the main tasks of the organization by a middle management jungle.

The *size* of the organization may be inappropriate to its mission. There has been much enthusiasm recently for making operational units smaller to avoid the problems of impersonality and alienation associated with large organizations. However, smaller is not always more beautiful; complex operations may need large numbers of people and specialist facilities to sustain them.

No organization can function without adapting to its *context*. This includes, obviously, the product market, fiscal policy and taxation. It is not always so obvious that the social context is equally important, especially the labour market.

Many organizational problems stem from job definition and rigidity. Those whose duties are precisely drawn are encouraged by that precision to view their range of activities as strictly delimited: ' that is not in my job description, so I will not do it'. This can be regarded as an uncooperative, bloody-minded attitude, but it is just as likely to be due to a concern not to infringe the area of someone else, or an anticipation of reprimand for exceeding responsibilities. When job descriptions are less precise, there is the danger that important matters will be overlooked, because responsibility is not defined, and members of the organization will do whatever they want to do rather than what they should do.

The correct assignment of decisions is ensuring that decisions to be made by individuals are so made, but that those to be made collectively are remitted to the appropriate body with the requisite authority to act. Is it a decision that needs individual flair and judgement, with the subsequent personal accountability that will result, or is it a decision that needs collective wisdom and consent to aid its subsequent implementation?

In the next two pages we have some suggestions for dealing with problems like these, but we need to reiterate the comment in chapter 12 about the importance of thoroughness. Getting the organization right and developing it to suit changing circumstances and changing personnel requires shrewd judgement and careful attention to details. It requires eternal vigilance also: organization is seldom 'right' for long.

The problem of over-management

A good indication of over-management lies in the steepness of the hierarchy, increasing the number of subordinates reporting to a single manager can flatten the hierarchy and reduce the problem.

1 How many tiers are there in the hierarchy ? Can any of these be removed?

2 Can some of the jobs defined as management be redefined as specialist or professional, so that they are taken out of the management direct line without any loss of status?

3 How much can the autonomy of the managed be increased? The greater the autonomy, the less need for supervision and the larger the number of people to be the responsibility of one manager.

4 Can the amount of target-setting be increased, so that the duties of employees are defined by output as well as method? This, too, will increase the number of people who can be the responsibility of one manager.

5 Can members of the organization achieve social status by other means than their managerial rank? To a large extent the steepness of the hierarchy is a product of social pressure to improve career prospects and enhance status. If there are alternative sources of those rewards, the social pressure is reduced.

The problem of size

Organizations tend to become more bureaucratic as they grow, and to steepen the hierarchy, with associated difficulties about morale among members of the organization distant from the centre. However, organizational growth does provide career growth and opportunities for changes of job among organization members.

1 Is there any part of the work of the organization that could safely be detached, either as a separate, autonomous organizational unit, or as a set of requirements placed on an external supplier? This could reduce organizational size, but are there potential problems that would outweigh the advantages, such as loss of control, security, etc?

2 Do you make the best use of consultants to avoid the need to increase the size of your organization, or are you in danger of becoming dependent on them?

3 Do you get the type of service you require from all your suppliers, or would you get better integration of some services by setting up your own specialist department within your own business?

4 In order to overcome the problems of low morale among organization members distant from the centre, are there ways in which operating units within the organization structure can be made more autonomous?

The problem of context

Strategic objectives can be more ambitious if the setting is buoyant, or competitive, and organization members will be more creative if the setting is changing and presenting challenges.

1 Does the way in which jobs within the organization are organized provide the range of opportunities, challenges and responsibility that general social developments are causing members of the organization to expect?

2 Are the various boundary roles in the organization set up in a way that provides the optimum interface between internal activities and the external context?

The problem of job rigidity

Apart from the problem of rigidity already mentioned, the main difficulty of job definition is where there is the possibility of overlap or omission.

1 Are there any activities within the organization where there is uncertainty about who has the responsibility? Can this uncertainty be usefully clarified?

2 Where there are job descriptions, do job holders regard them as a useful framework for their contribution, as a straitjacket limiting their scope, or as irrelevancies? If they are a straitjacket, can they be altered? If they are irrelevant, can they be thrown away?

3 Do job holders write their own job descriptions or have them written by someone else? If they are written by the job holders they are probably useful; if written by someone else they could be useless.

The problem of decisions

Decisions can go wrong because they are taken too hastily, or because they are taken too late and an opportunity has been missed. Much depends on how the matter requiring decision is presented to the decision maker(s).

1 Are collective decisions made on matters requiring a range of expertize, or where implementation of the decision may be difficult because of employee resistance? This type of decision normally should not be taken by an individual.

2 Are individual decisions made on matters that are straightforward, with policy precedents or procedural guidance, those needing very specialized experience or flair, and those matters on which individual accountability is important? This type of decision normally should not be taken collectively.

3 Does the organization have a convention whereby people are encouraged to decide quickly when a matter would be considered better at length?

4 Does the decision-making convention encourage prevarication?

Exercises

1 Sketch out your organization chart and check it for over-management:

   a Can any of the jobs where the title includes the word 'manager' have that element removed without a loss of status by the job holder and with an improvement to organizational efficiency?

   b Can you reduce the number of hierarchical levels?

   c Is there scope for increasing the autonomy of job holders?

   If your answer is "yes" to any of the above questions, sketch an improved organization chart and summarize the benefits it will provide.

2 Is your organization too big or too small? How can you move it to a more appropriate size?

3 In what ways is your organization not properly attuned to the setting in which it operates?

4 To what extent does slack job definition need to be tightened up and to what extent is job definition too rigid?

5 Jot down 10 decisions that you can recall from the recent past that were dubious. Could any of them have been made better by different organization?

Further reading

CHILD J. *Organization*. 2nd ed, London, Harper and Row, 1984
   Chapter 3 is particularly appropriate to the question of over-management and the span of control.
KHANDWALLA P N. *Design of Organisations*. New York, Harcourt, Brace, Jovanovich, New York, 1977
   This book contains detailed and extensive suggestions about how to identify problems of organization.

And finally . . .

It is not possible to predict the exact outcome of any initiative in organizational design or organizational change. There are always unintended consequences.

16 Analyzing your network of contacts

Managers spend a lot of time talking to other people. Who they talk to is important as it effects what influences are brought to bear on the decisions and actions that result from these conversations. Some contacts will be made because of the formal relations between job titles but a lot of contacts are because of the manager's personal network of people. Another person doing the same job would have a different network.

Organizational contacts can be described in two ways; hierarchies and networks. Hierarchies are characterized by the organization chart that outlines the formal relations between members of a particular organization. The chart tells us the formal distribution of power and authority, who reports to whom, the approved channels of communication, links between sections and also something of how the work is organized. This statement of the hierarchy takes us from the macro level of organization structure to the micro level of individual contacts within the organization.

Work by Kotter has demonstrated that individual managers will also have a network of contacts. He found that this was different from, but consistent with, the formal organization structure. Networks are cooperative relationships with people who can help one accomplish things. They are subordinates, peers, outsiders, the boss's boss, subordinate's subordinate or anyone on whom one is dependent to get things done. These networks are often large. Kotter's general managers included hundreds or thousands of people, and every relationship is different. The network is for sharing ideas, information and resources. It gives particularly the horizontal link not prescribed in the organizational chart. Networks include 'knowing how the system works'.

Contacts are created and maintained by the whole range of interpersonal behaviours. Some will be personal friends made in previous jobs or at college. Others will be new contacts made because they are politically necessary. A manager's network is not the same as the old boy system. The difference is that the old boy system is protecting the self interest of a limited few whereas the network is widespread and essential to get things done.

This chapter is rather different from the others. It consists of an exercise designed to help you bring together ideas from several other chapters and how they effect you and your job. We ask you to look at both the formal and informal contacts at work and analyze whether they need improving. This interpersonal contact is the main theme of the first three sections of this book. Some chapters deal with why it is important to make the contact such as chapters 12, 13, 20 and 22, others help with how to make the contact more effective, for example chapters 5, 7 and 24.

The organization chart

Draw a personal organization chart, with yourself at the centre, using ☐ to indicate job positions and showing the names of those currently holding those posts. The chart should include formal relations you have inside and outside the organization. The circle represents the organization boundary. On the right is an example of a typical organization chart.

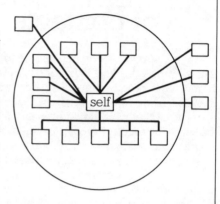

The network of contacts

On a second chart list all the individuals or groups who can affect how effective you are in your job, but with whom you do not have a formal working relationship included in the first chart. Give both names and positions. The drawing, which may look something like the one on the right, will illustrate your informal network.

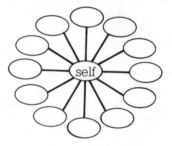

Evaluating the network of contacts

Use the form opposite to rank order the contacts, formal and informal, in their importance to you in getting your job done effectively.

Rate each contact on a scale between -3 and $+3$, according to how helpful the person is to you.

What can be done to improve communication with those you have rated between -1 and -3 ?

rank	contact	−3	−2	−1	0	+1	+2	+3	suggested improvement
1									
2									
3									
4									
5									
6									

Improving the network of contacts

Use the charts opposite to help you analyze whether there is anyone who should be in your network but is not yet. These can be added to the list of people with whom you need to improve communication.

Having identified the people, think about which is the most appropriate method for each of them. There are various strategies listed below but you might also find chapters 5, 6, 7, 13 and 24 helpful.

Kotter found that the general managers created networks by:

- focussing on people they felt dependent upon or who were necessary to get things done;

- making others feel obliged to them;

- encouraging others to identify with them;

- establishing their reputation;

- making others feel dependent on them;

- replacing incompetent subordinates;

- changing suppliers and other outsiders;

- shaping the environment to encourage teamwork through structures, systems and processes.

Exercises

1 The centre pages of this chapter are organized as an exercise. There are various ways of using it. You can use it to analyze your network at work. Alternatives would be to consider your last job and compare it with your present one; think about the people you know socially and the access they give you to a variety of different activities and ideas; or, if you are not currently in employment, what contacts do you have formally through your last employment, school or college and informally that might help in finding employment?

2 List those people you talk to in the next week at work. Was the outcome satisfactory or not? Why?

3 What useful purpose do business lunches serve?

4 Is social skills training appropriate for managers or does it just reinforce a cultural superiority?

Further reading

FERGUSON M. *Aquarian Conspiracy*. Los Angeles, Calif., J P Tarcher, 1980
KOTTER J P. *The General Managers*. New York, The Free Press, 1982
NAISBITT J. *Megatrends*. London, Macdonald, 1982

And finally . . .

Ferguson *op cit* notes that networking is done by

'conferences, phone calls, air travel, books, phantom organizations, papers, pamphleteering, photocopying, lectures, workshops, parties, grapevines, mutual friends, summit meetings, coalitions, tapes, newsletters'.

17 Organizational communication

The problems of organizational communication are so extensive and so difficult that it can be regarded as one of management's major challenges. It is the flow of information through the organization structure, both formal and informal, that can produce understanding and action or mistrust and inefficiency. As the information flows it produces a reaction and affects working relationships and individual performance, so that the information is used to exchange ideas, attitudes and feelings.

The purposes of organizational communication are first general information, which keeps members of the organization advised of matters of general interest that will affect their interest in the organization and the degree of their commitment to its affairs: progress reports, news about fresh initiatives, orders won, people appointed and so forth. Hard information is more specific as it is required by individuals from others to shape their own activities. The designer needs a great deal of hard information from the market place and from the production department to ensure that detailed design work meets the demands and difficulties of both areas. Authorization is what members of the organization seek in order to trigger a part of the administrative process, ranging from permission to engage a new employee to the acceptance of a departmental budget, or taking a day's leave for a funeral. Instruction is the form of communication that tells people what to do and, sometimes, how to do it.

All of these will be influenced in their style and effectiveness, by the organizational culture, so that a culture which encourages openness and trust is likely to produce plenty of general information and a ready compliance with instructions, but the main factor for us to consider here is structure and methods. If the structure of the organization puts groups in competition with each other, it will also impair the quality of communication between those groups; if it makes them mutually dependent, it will improve the quality of intergroup communication. Which is more appropriate in the situation, the cohesion and concern for task accomplishment within the groups that will be engendered by rivalry, or the collaboration and free flow of communication that will come from their mutual dependency?

The formal communications structure is represented in the pattern of working relationships and reporting, the procedures and administrative drills, the minutes of committees, the forms, the books of rules and the works of reference. The informal communications structure is to some extent the flesh on the bones of formality; it is the telephone conversations, the chats over coffee, encounters in the corridors and the confidential briefings. Although not usually 'official' these exchanges are effective at turning information into understanding and increase the number of outlets through which information passes. A significant part of the informal structure is the networks that each individual manager sets up, as we saw in chapter 2.

Communications media

1 *The organization chart* specifies working relationships and thus identifies sources of authorization and instruction, as well as sources of hard information. Does your chart include names, telephone numbers and office locations to aid communication?

2 *Procedures and drills* show people how things should be done and specify what information is required by whom and for what purpose. Does your organization culture encourage the use or the avoidance of procedures?

3 *Reports and statements* are standardized ways of supplying factual information to a large number of people, like the monthly statement of personal earnings, deductions and cumulative pay, or the monthly performance indicators or the annual report to shareholders.

4 *Written messages* are a different form of communication as they are usually complementary to some interpersonal communication, so that their purpose is to prepare for the interpersonal exchange or to confirm its outcome: a draft report, the agenda for a meeting, the letter of invitation to an employment interview and the training manual are examples. Written messages are seldom sufficient to bring about a change in behaviour by the recipient. Do you ever rely on a written message for action only to find that the action is not taken?

5 *Electronic mail* is a way of speeding up the transmission of many written messages and reducing the number that are stored after receipt.

6 *Word of mouth* means people speaking to each other, which remains the preferred mode of communication for most matters by most people. This is not just for informal communication, but also for many formal aspects, like briefing groups, negotiations, job instruction and discipline. It is a method that provides the maximum opportunity for feedback, which is an essential ingredient of all communication. The telephone can be a fair substitute, as feedback is possible, but electronic mail is a very poor substitute for face to face exchange.

Communications and status

Those carrying high status in situations are encouraged to be cautious and bland in their comments about matters of high uncertainty. Their listeners will not allow them tc speculate, as the need for certainty will cause them to interpret speculation as commitment. The person with little status in the organization can say "I think we will have to close down" and then engage in discussion. The person with high status could not make that statement without it being interpreted as "We are going to close down". High status can impede and distort the feedback you receive. It can also turn casual thoughts into policy commitments.

The team briefing approach

Briefing groups are a way of using the formal organization structure to ensure regular face to face discussion between managers and their subordinates about matters of importance to the subordinates in their contribution to organizational success. The manager always briefs teams of subordinates rather than individuals so that a team sense is developed and contributions to the discussion will be informative to all because of the range of the interests and perspectives present. The 'cascade' principle is that the person at the top of the hierarchy briefs immediate subordinates, who then hold separate briefings of their own subordinates, and so on.

1 People are briefed collectively to enrich the information exchange.

2 The cascade idea involves a development of the briefing so that the opening message or issue is reinterpreted to be relevant to the needs of the listeners.

3 Meetings are regular (usually at fortnightly or quarterly periods) and with a regular agenda, like the examination of a series of performance indicators.

4 Although the meetings are for two-way communication, and the briefing manager will listen and respond as well as conveying information, their purpose is briefing, not general discussion, dodging issues or airing grievances.

Some problems of organizational communication

1 *Hierarchical levels* can distort messages that are relayed through too many intermediaries. Remember how the message 'Send reinforcements, we're going to advance' became 'Send three and fourpence, we're going to a dance.'

2 *Selective perception* is the problem of our expectations leading us to hear what we expect or want to hear rather than what is intended.

3 The *credibility* of the message sender will influence the belief of the recipients in the message they receive and the action they take as a result.

4 *Information overload* is a problem mainly of written communication. Few people have the time or inclination to read long messages thoroughly and will either look for a summary (like newspaper headlines) or will ask someone else to give them the gist of what the message contains.

Exercises

1 For which of the following would you use only formal methods, only informal, or a combination of both formal and informal communication:

   a Advising employees of the date of closing down for Christmas

   b A change in the annual holiday entitlement

   c Proposals for a merger with another company

   d A new procedure for claiming travel expenses

   e Changed safety regulations

2 An American study of the accuracy of messages being transmitted from the top to the bottom of the hierarchy in 100 companies, found that vice presidents understood 67 per cent of what they heard from directors, but the percentage then declined from 56 per cent by plant managers, 30 per cent by supervisors and 20 per cent on the shop floor. How could team briefing improve this accuracy?

Further reading

MEGGINSON L C, MOSLEY D C, and PIETRI P H. *Management*. New York, Harper International, 1983, chapter 11

ALLEN R K. *Organizational Management through Communications*. London, Harper and Row, 1977

THOMSON F. 'The Seven Deadly Sins of Briefing Groups' in *Personnel Management*. February 1983

And finally . . .

In 1799 Napoleon Bonaparte was leading his troops in the Middle East. 1,200 Turks had been captured at Jaffa and Napoleon, it is said, was asked what should be done with them. Seized with a sudden fit of coughing, he said "Ma sacre toux!" (My damned cough). His chief of staff understood him to say "Massacrez tous!" (Massacre them all) and ordered the immediate execution of the 1,200.

At the battle of Balaclava in 1854 the British Commander sent the order to his cavalry:

"Advance and take advantage of any opportunity to recover the heights. You will be supported by infantry which have been ordered to advance on two fronts."

In transmission the order was distorted so that the last sentence read:

"You will be supported by infantry which have been ordered. Advance on two fronts."

The result was the infamous, futile Charge of the Light Brigade.

18   Group-working

Working in an organization involves working not only as an individual but also as a member of a group. Some of these groups will be permanent, others will be formed to deal with particular tasks. Some understanding of how groups work is useful whether as a manager of a group or a member of a group.

There are several reasons why we need to have groups at work. Some tasks are performed better, or can be done only by groups of people working together. With increasing complexity of the demands on organizations no one person has all the information so groups are necessary to bring together all the required expertize to get things done. Belonging to a group can stimulate each person to greater or better effort and tends to increase job satisfaction and morale. Also, people will support that which they have helped to create, so participation in group decision-making can have useful consequences for the implementation of decisions. Working in a group provides the social satisfaction we all seek by forming informal groups.

In all human interaction there are two elements, *content* and *process*. The first deals with the subject matter or task of the interaction. The second describes how the interaction is done, how things are communicated, by whom and when. It includes the answers to such questions as: "Who participates?", "How do they influence others?", "What norms of behaviour are there in the group?", and "How are decisions arrived at?" Most of us concentrate on the content of group workings but attention to the process is extremely valuable as it is often process problems that lead to ineffective group working. This chapter and the following two are concerned with the process side of group working. The final test of an effective group is how well the task is carried out.

Effective groups have various features that distinguish them from ineffective groups. The members function as a unit with people seeing themselves as members of a team. They work for a common purpose and participate fully in the group effort. Within the group, all the skills and materials necessary to do the task are present. They talk a lot. This and the following chapters suggest ways of fostering important features. The clue that a group is successful is the use of phrases with the word 'we' in them. The process of becoming an effective group takes time, and Tuckman (see the following page) has described the stages groups go through to increase cohesion and performance. The length of time taken for this process will vary, in direct proportion to the time the group is expected to work together. If it is a permanent group, the investment is higher so everybody needs to ensure their position in the group more clearly than in a temporary group. Thus, it may take the permanent group months to go through the various stages and minutes for the one-off meeting.

Observing, analyzing and improving the process side of group working will achieve more satisfactorily and effectively the task of the group.

Stages in the growth of group cohesion and performance

Stage of development	Process	Outcome
1 Forming	There is anxiety, dependence on leader, testing to find out the nature of the situation and what behaviour is acceptable	Members find out what the task is, what the rules are and what methods are appropriate
2 Storming	Conflict between sub-groups, rebellion against leader, opinions are polarized, resistance to control by group	Emotional resistance to demands of task
3 Norming	Development of group cohesion, norms emerge, resistance is overcome and conflicts patched up; mutual support and sense of group identity	Open exchange of views and feelings; cooperation develops
4 Performing	Interpersonal problems are resolved; interpersonal structure becomes the means of getting things done; roles are flexible and functional	Solutions to problems emerge; there are constructive attempts to complete tasks and energy is now available for effective work

Based on B W TUCKMAN *Development Sequences in Small Groups, pp 384–99 op cit*

Types of communication networks in groups

The pattern of communications in groups can have important consequences for efficiency and member satisfaction. The patterns can vary in the number of potential channels available, the equality of the communication possible and how centralized the pattern is. Different patterns are effective for different tasks. Some common patterns, based on the researches of Leavitt, are shown below.

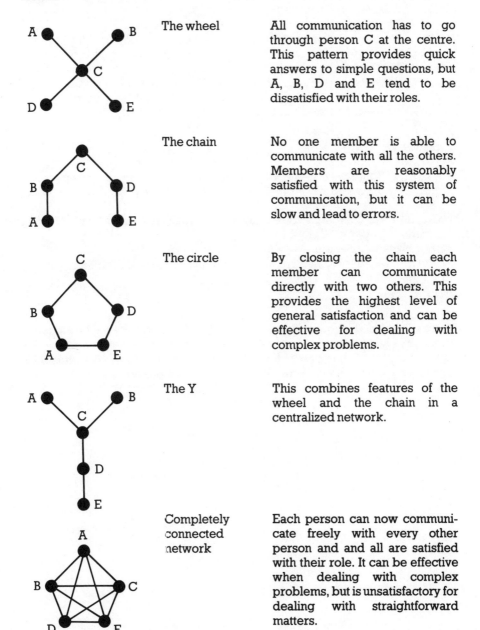

The wheel

All communication has to go through person C at the centre. This pattern provides quick answers to simple questions, but A, B, D and E tend to be dissatisfied with their roles.

The chain

No one member is able to communicate with all the others. Members are reasonably satisfied with this system of communication, but it can be slow and lead to errors.

The circle

By closing the chain each member can communicate directly with two others. This provides the highest level of general satisfaction and can be effective for dealing with complex problems.

The Y

This combines features of the wheel and the chain in a centralized network.

Completely connected network

Each person can now communicate freely with every other person and and all are satisfied with their role. It can be effective when dealing with complex problems, but is unsatisfactory for dealing with straightforward matters.

Exercises

1 Think of a group you have worked with that you enjoyed belonging to. List five reasons why this was so. Now think of a group you found frustrating to work with. List five reasons why.

2 When you are next in a meeting or group that has recently formed, try to find two examples of behaviour that indicate which stage the group has reached: forming, storming, norming or performing.

3 Using a puzzle book or crossword from the paper, get a group of five or six people and experiment with the patterns of communication on the previous page. For example 'the wheel' has a central figure who is the only person the others can speak to; with 'the circle' only the adjacent person is addressed. At the end of the exercise ask how each person felt about the different groups. Time the problem-solving to see which was most effective.

Further reading

LEAVITT H J. "Some aspects of certain communication patterns on group performance" in *Journal of Abnormal and Social Psychology*. 45, No 1, pp 38–50, 1951

TUCKMAN B W. "Development Sequences in small groups" in *Psychological Bulletin*. 63, pp 384–99, 1965

HUNT J. *Managing People at Work*. London, Pan, 1979

SCHEIN E H. *Organisational Psychology*. London, Prentice Hall, 1965

And finally . . .

Norms develop in groups as to what is expected and accepted from each member. These expectations about each other's contributions develop from a convergence of perceptions of each other's roles. These norms then influence the future behaviour of the members of the group.

19 Analysis of team roles

There are two aspects to group working: content and process. These are also reflected in the roles played by members of a team. For teams to continue and work well, both task oriented and social/emotional oriented behaviours are necessary. Task oriented behaviours are those which concentrate on getting things done, such as asking questions, suggesting things, or giving possible solutions. Social/emotional behaviours are those which look after the process of the group by such methods as supporting other people's views, releasing tension through jokes, or nodding agreement. Equally, there are behaviours that are disruptive to completing the task or maintaining an agreeable social/emotional environment to work in.

Bales (1950) developed a series of observation categories (see the following page) for studying the process of interaction in small groups. He found that teams needed members who kept things moving towards the goal in a coordinated way, and other members to ensure that relationships remained sufficiently harmonious for individuals to continue contributing to the group or team. This model has been developed by Belbin (1981), who concluded that there were eight roles needed in effective management teams apart from specialist and functional roles. The eight roles are:

- *Company worker*, who keeps the organization's interests to the fore;

- *Chairman*, who ensures all views are heard and keeps things moving;

- *Shaper*, who influences by argument and by following particular topics;

- *Ideas person*, who contributes novel suggestions;

- *Resource investigator*, who evaluates whether contributions are practical and finds out where and how to get the resources;

- *Monitor/evaluator*, who assesses whether contributions are valid and to what extent the team is meeting its objectives;

- *Team worker*, who maintains the group process by joking or agreeing;

- *Completer/finisher*, who tries to get things done and suggests conclusions.

As the range of technical skills and backgrounds become more diverse, team working becomes increasingly important. Understanding the ways in which teams work is the best way to work effectively with and through them; particularly when there is no possibility of making changes to the teams. By analyzing the roles that members fill, to see what contributions are being made and what is left out, team leaders can make their teams more effective. This analysis can also provide the basis for developing the contributions and career prospects of individual team members. The types of activity will vary with different teams and situations, but some typical activities are the way people handle informal and formal meetings, telephone conversations and the type of memo they write. These will tell you which of the various roles they are performing. Most people fill more than one role, but usually a consistent pattern emerges. It is useful for the team leader to analyze the roles team members are filling, first to analyze their behaviours, and secondly to find out whether there are any roles not filled.

Interaction process categories

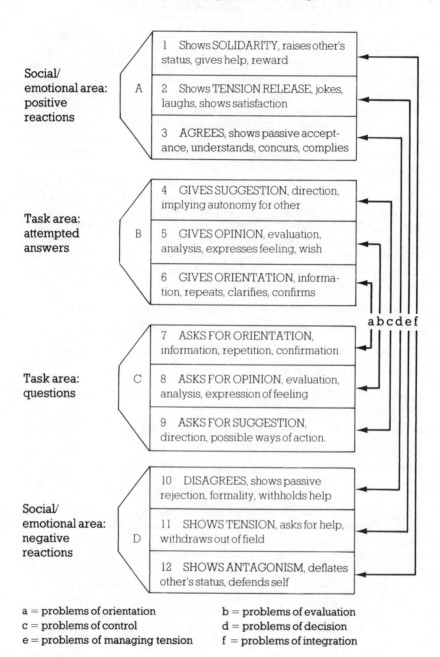

Social/emotional area: positive reactions

A
1 Shows SOLIDARITY, raises other's status, gives help, reward
2 Shows TENSION RELEASE, jokes, laughs, shows satisfaction
3 AGREES, shows passive acceptance, understands, concurs, complies

Task area: attempted answers

B
4 GIVES SUGGESTION, direction, implying autonomy for other
5 GIVES OPINION, evaluation, analysis, expresses feeling, wish
6 GIVES ORIENTATION, information, repeats, clarifies, confirms

Task area: questions

C
7 ASKS FOR ORIENTATION, information, repetition, confirmation
8 ASKS FOR OPINION, evaluation, analysis, expression of feeling
9 ASKS FOR SUGGESTION, direction, possible ways of action.

Social/emotional area: negative reactions

D
10 DISAGREES, shows passive rejection, formality, withholds help
11 SHOWS TENSION, asks for help, withdraws out of field
12 SHOWS ANTAGONISM, deflates other's status, defends self

a b c d e f

a = problems of orientation   b = problems of evaluation
c = problems of control   d = problems of decision
e = problems of managing tension f = problems of integration

NAMES							
SOLIDARITY							
TENSION RELEASE							
AGREES							
GIVES SUGGESTION							
GIVES OPINION							
GIVES ORIENTATION							
ASKS FOR ORIENTATION							
ASKS FOR OPINION							
ASKS FOR SUGGESTION							
DISAGREES							
SHOWS TENSION							
SHOWS ANTAGONISM							

1   Put the names of team members across the top.

2   When you observe any member demonstrating any of the behaviours on the left put a stroke 1 in the appropriate box.

3   At the end of the period, meeting or week, analyze which role each member plays most frequently and which roles are not met.

4   The same sort of observation form could be used with Belbin's managerial roles.

Exercises

1 Use the form on the previous page in your next meeting.

2 In your next meeting, adopt a behaviour pattern that you do not normally use, either by talking a lot or not at all, or by adopting one of the behaviours in Bales's list. What was the effect?

3 Is there any difference between a committee and a team?

4 Will some of Bales's behaviours be more useful in the forming and storming phases than in the norming and performing phases of a group's working? If so, which?

5 Think of two groups you belong to. Do you play the same role in each?

6 Which of Belbin's eight management roles do you play? What about your boss? Who is the team worker and how is he or she treated?

Further reading

BALES R F. *Interaction Process Analysis*. London, Addison Wesley, 1950

BELBIN R M, ASTON B R and MOTTRAM R D. "Building Effective Management Teams" in *Journal of General Management*. 2, p 23–9, 1976

HANDY C. *Understanding Organisations*. 2nd ed, Harmondsworth, Middx., Penguin, 1981

STEWART A and V. *Tomorrow's Manager Today*. 2nd ed, London, IPM, 1981

And finally . . .

'Groups fit well with a democratic culture, with representative systems of government. Participation and involvement go well with assumptions of man as an independent individual . . . But let us not be mesmerised. Let us realise that a proper understanding of groups will demonstrate how difficult they are to manage.'

HANDY C, *Understanding Organisations, op cit* p 173

20 Committees

Committees are a specialized form of group working. They have relatively formal meetings to deal with matters that are too complex, too demanding or too risky for an individual to handle alone. They also provide a way of consulting with others. Blau and Scott (1963) list the main reasons why committees are used:

a The sifting of suggestions in social interaction helps to correct errors.
b Thinking is helped by the social support that comes from interaction.
c Competition among members for respect mobilizes their energies for contribution to the task.

Committee members both compete and cooperate. Although sharing the common purpose in the aim of the committee itself, they have differing personal interests and aspirations in their committee work, often competing for a share of limited resources that the committee has at its disposal. This competition can raise the level of achievement of the group by putting everyone on their mettle.

Committee members cooperate both in factions and as a whole. A faction is an alliance between some individuals to improve their competitive edge eg "Will you support me on this, if I support you on that?". The committee will operate as a whole when competition is resolved eventually by a consensus in which individual objections or reservations are withdrawn in favour of a cooperative strategy after the competing views have been aired.

The method of committee discussion is to exchange information and then to work on hypotheses. On each agenda item members first seek out the facts, even if those facts do not necessarily support their personal cause. The discussion then moves to consider alternative hypotheses, which are developed both by endorsement and critical analysis. The chairperson will look for the most acceptable in order to single it out for the committee's consent.

The main problem of committees is that they take more time than most people willingly give, and the quality of decisions may be poor. Five people meeting for two hours take 10 working hours to reach a decision, which one person might have done better working alone for five hours – or five minutes. However, this type of reservation ignores the importance of decision implementation. Five people after the meeting are committed to make work a decision that they understand already: the solo decision maker has to win commitment by time-consuming explanation. Uncertainty about the quality of decisions is based on an assumption that the need for committee members to compromise will lead to decisions that are safe rather than adventurous. This, however, has not been proven by research.

The best size of committee will depend on its main purpose. Too few can lead to insufficient input of information and ideas; too many leads to unwieldly discussion, diverse information input and inhibiting of the less confident members. Large committees are preferred where the main purpose is to brief the members or where widely different talents and experience are needed to make decisions. Small committees are preferred where speedy decision on complex matters is needed, or where the matter under discussion is to be kept confidential.

Guidance notes for committee chairman

Before the meeting

1 What is the meeting for – decision-making, briefing, generating ideas, or something else?

2 Review papers for the meeting to consider timing and pacing

3 Review meeting arrangements with secretary

During the meeting

4 Introduce new members

5 Call for apologies and minutes of last meeting.

6 Introduce agenda items

7 Call on members to speak, seeking a balance of views, style and authority

8 Focus discussion on disagreements that must be resolved

9 Periodically summarize discussion and point a new direction

10 Ask for clarification from a member whose comments others find puzzling or unacceptable

11 Pick a workable hypothesis from the discussion and choose the right time to put it to the meeting for acceptance

12 Finish on time

After the meeting

13 Check with secretary that the notes or minutes of the meeting are drafted, agreed with you, and circulated

14 Ensure that those who have to take action know what to do, and do it

15 Review your role as chairman; what will you do differently next time?

Guidance notes for committee member

Before the meeting

1 What is the meeting for? (see 1 left)

2 What is your role – sage, brake, synthesizer, diplomat, delegate, adviser, stimulus, or something else?

3 Review papers for meeting and notes you plan to use

4 Check that you have taken the action agreed for you at last meeting

During the meeting

5 Use social skills to persuade others

6 Be objective in seeking solutions that will be acceptable to others

7 Avoid personal attacks on others that would isolate you from other members

8 Support and develop contributions by others that you regard as constructive and potentially acceptable after modification

9 Constantly monitor the mood of the meeting to judge when best to make your contributions – facts, opinions, suggestions or hypotheses

10 Always 'work through the chair', recognizing the authority that the group always invests in that role

After the meeting

11 Consult with those you represent to advise them of committee decisions and required action

12 Study the minutes, when circulated, noting corrections needed and consider suggestions for future agenda items

13 Take action on those items requiring your action

14 Review your participation; what will you do differently next time?

Guidance notes for committee secretary
(These notes assume that the committee meets monthly on Day 28)

Day

Minutes and preliminaries
1,2 Draft minutes, including notes of action items
5 Clear minutes with chairman and confirm date of next meeting
6,7 Type, copy and distribute minutes
7 Book room for next meeting

Agenda
12 Ask committee members for items to be included on next agenda
16 Discuss agenda items and sequence with chairman
Suggested sequence:
a Introduction of new members; apologies for absence
b Minutes of previous meeting reviewed for accuracy
c Matters arising from minutes and not appearing on agenda
d Items for decision and causing little controversy
e Most difficult item
f Next most difficult item
g Items requiring discussion but not decision
h Easy items
i Any other business
j Provisional date for next meeting

Run-up
19 Circulate agenda and other papers
23 Check room arrangements
27 Collate all papers, past minutes, apologies

The meeting
28 a Supply papers to chairman in agenda sequence
b Take general notes of discussion in order to provide information, if needed, on earlier points as meeting proceeds
c Take precise notes of matters agreed and of who is to take action
d Remain detached from discussion except for providing information or seeking clarification

The main art of *chairing* a committee is in maintaining a balance between the stimulus of competition and a reasonably secure, agreeable atmosphere for discussion. Competition between members must not reach a point where it destroys the possibility of cooperation and making progress.

The best *committee members* are essential to the purpose and not people who might be useful. They should be interested in its purpose, with some stake in its success, and should have relevant knowledge and experience. They should have enough time to attend and prepare for meetings.

Exercises

1 The next time you attend a committee meeting, see if your fellow committee members can be categorized in the way suggested by our guidance notes on the previous page: sage, brake, synthesizer, diplomat, delegate, adviser, stimulus. Is there an important role missing? Is there a good balance, or are too many people filling one or two roles? Does the committee need a change of membership?

2 At a meeting concentrate your own mode of participation in the form suggested in the guidance notes on the previous page (4–12 for chairman, 5–10 for members). What effect did your change of mode have?

3 President J F Kennedy is alleged to have said about committees: 'Everyone is the father of success; failure is an orphan.' Think through the committees which you attend and identify the ways in which the number of orphans can be reduced.

Further reading

BLAU P M and SCOTT W R. 'Processes of Communication in Formal Organizations' in Argyle M (ed) *Social Encounters*. Harmondsworth, Middx., Penguin Books, 1976
SCHWARTZ D F. *Introduction to Management: Principles, Practices and Processes*. New York, Harcourt, Brace, Jovanovich, 1980
SMITH P B. *Groups within Organizations*. London, Harper and Row, 1973
SUMMERS I and WHITE D E. 'Creativity Techniques: Towards Improvement in the Decision Process' in *The Academy of Management Review*. April 1976

And finally . . .

The main forms of committee are first *the plural executive*, a decision-making body of people who all carry a share of responsibility individually and who can make a collective decision through all having a stake in the matters being discussed.

Secondly, *the linking pin* is a group with the purpose of keeping people in a complex organization informed about what is happening. Members with varied responsibilities come to brief others, to be briefed, and to take away messages for others.

Thirdly, *the think tank* is a group of people who serve an advisory purpose by working out strategies and rough-cut decisions for others to accept, reject or modify before taking action.

21   Dealing with change

Change has become so much a part of our expectations both at work and in our private lives that we need to develop strategies to deal with it. Most of us are unsettled by uncertainty and try to control, predict and maintain things in their present state as this is more comfortable. Toffler (1970) argues that we are dazzled by change which we cannot understand and he maintains we need to have stability zones (see chapter 11 of this book) so we can deal with the change happening around us. In his later book Toffler argues (1980) that we are now less terrified of change and are beginning to deal more successfully with it.

Managers not only need to deal with change at the personal level but also need to be influencing what changes are to happen and occasionally to initiate change. These changes may be due to a variety of reasons: competitive position, reducing expenditure, more efficient, easier, pleasanter, change in personnel, change in available resources, political pressure, outside influences, internal reasons or purely personal factors. Having analyzed why a change is necessary managers need to decide what change to make and how to implement it. Changes can be anything from major reorganizations where most members have their work changed or removed, to small changes in procedure. All changes need careful consideration to ensure that the desired effect of change has the maximum chance of happening.

Managers not only need to influence what changes are to happen but frequently have to deal with change imposed from elsewhere. This is when both the reasons for change, what changes and how are decided elsewhere. Managers, usually middle or junior management, are left with the job of implementing change they have not taken part in deciding and may not agree with. Getting subordinates to comply, who in turn have not been involved in the decision-taking nor necessarily agree with the changes, is one of the more difficult and challenging tasks of management. Particularly where the change is one of rationalization, reduction and retrenchment after a period of uncertainty.

Dealing with change also has a political aspect. Those who can deal with uncertainty and find the solution are the more powerful. Where this also involves some prediction of how the future might be, power is even greater. This power becomes authority by being legitimized through increased status being given to those who forecast and plan for change. Some may have expertize in the area and so become authorities; others are those with job titles higher up the hierarchy and in authority. There is an interaction whereby those with authority claim the right to determine what changes are made and those who deal with change become authorities. Consequently, it is important for managers to deal with change because it is intrinsically linked with their role as managers.

Managers have two choices: they can let change happen to them with all the anxiety of uncertainty, or they can deal with change and influence some of the change taking place. Either way, change cannot be ignored.

Why make a change?

Are you sure the change you are suggesting is useful? Is it just a desire to make an impact for career reasons? What objectives or outcomes will be beneficial as a result of this change?

Do others agree that change is necessary?

Problem solving techniques (see chapter 8) are useful for analyzing what change might be useful.

Inventiveness is more likely when:
notes are kept of moments of insight which usually come in periods of rest after working hard on the problem;
deadlines and quotas are set which ensure people try to find solutions rather than putting off the problem till later;
time and place are set aside for generating ideas which otherwise would get squeezed out by other demands.
listening and rewarding innovative ideas within the department or organization.

Dissemination

Influencing and persuading other people that the idea is fruitful and is necessary to get things changed. (see part B of this book) They need to be persuaded that the proposal is not only new but an improved method.

It is necessary to get sufficient commitment that resources are made available, with a budget to evaluate the feasibility of the proposed change.

Implementing

Change is easier to implement if people see the change as in their interest and they are involved in the change. Those who have made the decision are committed to making it work.

There are three phases to change. Different people are better at managing each phase.
1 *Unfreeze*   people are made ready to learn
2 *Change*   the change or learning takes place
3 *Refreeze*   the change is consolidated

Participation

How one implements change will vary with the type of participation that is practised in the organization or department. In some the convention will be that there is extensive consultation to win consent for what is proposed; in others change will be implemented by decree. The figure below lists categories of consent sought in different organizations before implementing change.

Category of employee consent

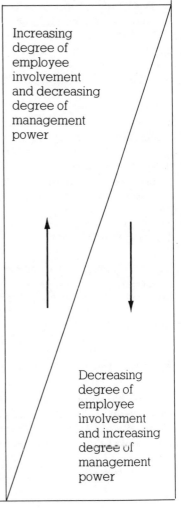

1 Controlling When there is employee control, as in a cooperative, managers are authorized to act by the employees.

2 Participative Employees do not control the business, but participate in decision-making on major issues.

3 Negotiated Employees limit the freedom of managers to introduce change through the separation of some matters on which action can be based only on some form of mutual accommodation.

4 Consultative Managers ask for the opinions of employees before implementing change, although the opinions may be partly or completely ignored.

5 Grudging Where managers are not willing to consult on decisions, or where unions are not strong enough to require consultation, there will be no explicit challenge from employees, but this does not necessarily mean commitment.

6 Normative In some organizations there is a strong sense of moral obligation to the leadership which is engendered among the employees. Any challenge or questioning would be unthinkable as it would imply a refutation of the shared values, or norms.

Increasing degree of employee involvement and decreasing degree of management power

Decreasing degree of employee involvement and increasing degree of management power

Consequences

All changes have consequences that are unintended as well as intended. Some of these are beneficial; others are not. Managers like to reduce to the minimum the unintended consequences of their change initiatives. It is worth spending time brainstorming (see chapter 31) to think of all the possible consequences of a proposed course of action

Exercises

1 Next time an idea is put to you, first list the reasons for rejecting it and then list the reasons for supporting it.

2 What types of uncertainty do other people present to you for resolution? Is this on the basis of expertize or position?

3 Try keeping a piece of paper with you at all times for the next week and whenever a potentially constructive thought comes to you write it down without evaluating it in any way. At the end of the week look through the list and see if there are any interesting ideas.

4 Who would you have to influence and persuade first if you wanted to change what you do at work?

5 In a period of change are you someone whose first instinct is to question the sense of the change or are you someone who enjoys constant change?

6 What sort of participation does your boss practise and what sort do you practise? One question to test this is to ask: "What are the consequences when those lower in the hierarchy disagree?"

Further reading

TOFFLER A. *Future Shock*. New York, Random House, 1970
TOFFLER A. *The Third Wave*. New York, Morrow, 1980
DRUCKER P F. *Managing in Turbulent Times*. London, Heinemann, 1980
STEWART V. *Change: the Challenge for Management*. Maidenhead, Berks., McGraw-Hill, 1983

And finally . . .

"No one knows in detail what the future holds or what will work best . . . For this reason we should think not of a single massive reorganization nor of a single revolutionary, cataclysmic change imposed from the top, but of thousands of conscious, decentralized experiments . . .'
Toffler, *The Third Wave, op cit*, p 452

C   Managing people

All managers have some sort of responsibility for the work of other people, which they have to organize or direct. Being able to command the respect of other people and get them to work effectively is not only a challenge for the managers themselves, but also an aspect of the managerial role that subordinates expect to be well done.

In this section of the book we deal first of all with how to set up a unit or section and make sure that the people in that unit have jobs that make sense to them and to you as a means of seeing the unit make its due contribution to the organization as a whole. We all spend our lives trying to understand the people around us, and there are no adequate substitutes for personal experience, but we offer some comments about understanding the people around you at work as well as an analysis of how power and authority operate in the organizational context.

Chapter 26 summarizes the method of using procedures as a means of mutual control, a sort of peace treaty whereby each party to the agreed procedure controls the behaviour of the other. This is distinct from the use of procedures in administrative action, which is considered at the opening of Part D.

Chapters 27 to 30 are all on familiar aspects of dealing with subordinates and handling the job of getting the best from your people at the same time as enabling them to get the best out of their jobs.

This section of the book closes with material on a specialized aspect of leading groups of people who have to work together to generate ideas and solutions to tricky problems: brainstorming.

Having used Part A to develop sound personal organization and Part B to come to terms with the ways organizational life functions, you now have the opportunity to develop a streamlined way to run your team in that context and make the most of your organizational skills.

22 Departmental organization

Chapters 12 to 17 dealt with the main questions of organization structure; this section examines how individual departments are organized. This is partly determined by the overall structure and philosophy, but individual employees often find their greatest frustration at the level of the department rather than the undertaking as a whole. Also, many of the exciting new developments that companies plan get into difficulty at the departmental level, through ineffective coordination of what individual employees and groups of employees actually do.

The work of people in departments is coordinated by various methods, the first being mutual adjustment, which is informal communication between a small group of people, like a family running a grocery or a pair of labourers fitting double-glazing. In a slightly larger unit there will be supervision, whereby one person is responsible for the work of a number of others, like the captain of an aircraft. A third method of coordination is to standardize the work to varying degrees. Automation is the extreme example, but most people work within some standardization, like the drills for administrative action described in chapter 32. Slightly different is the standardization of output, as in the specification to the skilled worker of the requirement, such as repairing a leaky valve, rather than specifying how the work should be done. The final method of coordination is to standardize skills; the close-knit social organization of the hospital operating theatre is largely achieved by the diverse skills of the individual team members, whose professional training then specifies their contribution. Most medical teams can work efficiently together even without knowing each other, because of this knowledge of the role that accompanies each skill.

The basis for departmentation in a business is seldom clearly thought out, and new departments are constantly being created to meet an assumed need or to satisfy the career aspirations of an individual. A systems department, for example, may be set up because there is the emerging function of data processing that needs specialist expertize. Otherwise there will be differing systems, inappropriate equipment specified, and general inefficiency. It is easy to set up the new department, but what other departments then need to be discontinued or have part of their function removed? Those questions are seldom asked. Similarly a new department may be created to give accelerated experience to some promising young executive who has to be blooded for major responsibility in a few years' time, but what may become redundant elsewhere in the organization as a result of that innovation?

We suggest overleaf a five stage process for either organizing a department from scratch or for identifying problems of organization in a long-standing department.

Five steps in departmental organization

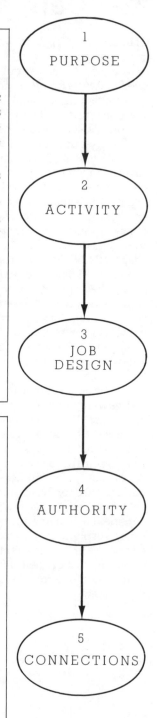

Step 1   What purpose will the department serve in the organization?

Is the purpose of the department to meet a basic business objective, like sales or purchasing, or is it in the hope that the organization will run more smoothly, like personnel? If the latter where are the savings to justify the innovation?

Has the new department been set up on the basis of outputs, like business objectives to be achieved, or is it based on inputs, like people and problems? If the latter, can outputs be produced to justify its existence? Are those outputs already being produced elsewhere in the organization?

Is the new department to deal with something that senior managers do not understand, like new pensions legislation, or something they find unattractive, like negotiating with trade union officials? If the answer is 'yes', are the reasons good enough?

Will the new department make problems of inter-departmental communication and coordination fewer or greater?

Step 2   What activities can be identified that will enable the department to meet its purpose?

Is the department grouping together those who share a particular skill, like word processor operating, or a particular responsibility, like quality assurance?

What are the activities to be carried out to meet the department's purpose? How many people with what types of experience and qualification are needed to undertake those activities?

How many ancillary employees, like errand boys and typists are needed? How can that number be reduced? How can it be reduced further still?

Are all the identified activities necessary? What do they take away from other departments? Will there be duplication? Is there a better way? Is the new department really needed?

Step 3 How are the activities of the department best grouped into jobs? (see also next chapter)

How much specialization is needed? Can some jobs be made more satisfying for the job holder by reducing the amount of specialization and increasing variety? Will that impair or enhance departmental efficiency? What degree of specialization is needed to maximize expertize without making the department too dependent on irreplaceable hyper-specialists?

Are boundaries between jobs clearly defined, or will there be arguments about who does what?

Will job holders have sufficient discretion to carry tasks through to completion, or will they be waiting constantly for other people and for decisions from others on matters they can satisfactorily resolve themselves?

Step 4 What formal authority do the job holders need delegated to them?

Are there job descriptions or other labels that indicate the authority that the job holder has to operate? Are there ways in which the labelling can authorize more effectively?

Do all job holders have the necessary equipment, like keys, and information, or computer codes, to carry out their duties within the department effectively?

Do all job holders have the necessary authorizations, like written permissions and authority to sign documents, that are needed for effective working in relation to other departments?

Are there any restrictions on the authority and autonomy of junior members of the department that exist only to provide symbolic status to senior members? If so, are they needed?

Step 5 How can the activities of job holders be connected through information systems and reporting?

How do job holders know what they need to know about the activities of their colleagues? Are there enough meetings to be informative but not so many that they become tiresome? Are there enough copies of memoranda and wastepaper baskets big enough to cope with them after they have been read, so that only essential material is filed? Are the possibilities of electronic mail fully utilized?

Is the physical location of individuals such as to aid communication between those who are constantly exchanging information?

Is there the best possible drill for routing papers and other material undergoing transformation by department members?

Is information that is withheld from job holders withheld of necessity?

Exercises

1 What is the purpose of your department and would that purpose be met better if there were more or fewer activities covered by it?

   Think about how you answered that question. Were any of the activities that you wanted to add included because you thought their addition would enhance your personal status or career prospects? If so, would their addition also improve the working of the entire organization? If their addition would not improve the working of the entire organization, how would your personal status and career prospects be affected? Were any of the activities you wanted to shed included because you find them boring or difficult? If so, what are the implications of their being moved elsewhere?

2 What features of the way your job is connected to others make you most dissatisfied? In the light of your answer, are there aspects of how your subordinates' jobs are interconnected that you will now modify?

3 If you have a private office, how much practical benefit does that confer apart from the satisfaction of privacy? If you do not have a private office, what benefits would you envisage from such a privilege? To what extent are your answers real and to what extent are they rationalizations?

Further reading

CHILD J. *Organization*. 2nd ed, London, Harper and Row, 1984
WILD R. *Work Organization*. London, John Wiley, 1975

And finally . . .

No department is very effective without good informal integration. The pensions department of a large business had on one occasion to send out 3,500 letters to employees. This was a tedious, routine job and it took a great deal of time because the details on each letter had to be carefully checked. Usually work of this nature is passed down to the most humble member of the staff, who resents the imposition, takes a long time over the job and makes mistakes. In this company all members of the department did it, working in the last half hour of the day every day for a week.

Not only was the job done quickly, it was done thoroughly. When there were subsequent enquiries from recipients of the letter, all members of the department could cope quickly with a range of questions through having had to understand completely the letter and all its implications. They had also been socially integrated by sharing in a single task, where they were all on an equal footing.

23 Job design

Who designed your job? You will probably say that it was not designed at all: it just exists. Most jobs have developed over quite a long period and in two different ways. First there is general development, so that sales assistant jobs have come into existence to meet broadly similar demands in different places and selling different things. Jobs like mechanic, typist, machinist, clerk, driver, managing director or ballet dancer all have similar characteristics or core elements. Secondly there is the way a job has been developed, and sometimes designed, in a particular situation, so that the job of coach driver has similar general characteristics in the local bus company as with an international tour operator, but the specific features of the two jobs are very different. Differences between similar jobs affect recruitment, training, payment and effectiveness. Few of those ideally suited to drive the school bus every morning would be as well suited to the same basic driving job, taking tourists to Turkey, and seldom would the same people apply for both jobs.

Job design is the process of getting the optimum fit between the organizational requirements from the individual employee and the individual's needs for satisfaction in doing the job. Because there are more jobs to be altered than thought out from scratch, it is sometimes described as *job redesign*.

Initially the management approach to job design was to make things as simple as possible for the employee to increase productive efficiency, following the theory that the simpler the task the quicker it could be completed. The extreme form of this idea was in mass production assembly lines where the complete task for an employee could be completed in as little as 45 to 60 seconds, with the same task being repeated 400 or 500 times a day. Increases in productive efficiency were impressive, but so were the increases in labour turnover, absenteeism, dissatisfaction, alienation, industrial action, sabotage and mental illness.

Attempts to mitigate the ill effects on employees were first concentrated only on the context of the work, such as the nature of supervision, the use of rest periods and attention to the ergonomic aspects of the workplace. Since 1959 initiatives have been made to alter the content of jobs, with great interest in how the nature of the job itself can motivate the job holder. To demonstrate success investigators have taken existing jobs and changed or redesigned them in order to compare performance before and after the change.

It is more practical to look at job design as the logical step to follow departmental organization. The third step of departmental organization suggested in the last chapter was 'How are the activities of the department best grouped into jobs?' By asking that question it is possible to design jobs that are coherent and whole, avoiding the artificial specialization that comes from merely making things simple. Job wholeness can produce departmental efficiency, economical staffing and satisfied employees.

Two well-known approaches to job redesign

1 *Job enlargement* extends the scope of jobs by combining two or more jobs into one, or by taking a number of work functions and putting them together in a single job with an increased variety and wholeness. The expansion is horizontal.

2 *Job enrichment* is a method that gives people more responsibility to set their own pace, decide their own methods and putting right their own mistakes, so increasing their autonomy. The expansion is vertical.

Job redesign is no panacea

The design of jobs has to be logical for organizational reasons as well as being an attempt to improve the lot of the employee, as enriched or enlarged jobs will only motivate those who seek personal fulfilment through work. That search, and the commitment that goes with it, will only be directed towards the job if the employee can see prospects of real personal growth by that means. The job that is made much better than it was still may not have enough potential for employees to seek fulfilment through work: they may continue to seek it outside work.

The American sociologist Harry Braverman believes that the labour process of the twentieth century has moved the planning and design of work tasks so irrevocably away from the employee and towards management that no change is possible without workers resuming control of their own work. If workers directed their own work it would not be possible to 'enforce upon them either the methodological efficiency or the working pace desired by capital.' The large scale rationalisation and de-skilling of first manual work, then clerical work and more recently management work through the computer, has removed skill, responsibility and control from the employee.

Few escape

Job design is not only an activity directed to the rank and file employee. A research study of management in American companies well known for management development included the comment:

'. . . . management in the typical organization was characterized by having rather narrow jobs and very tightly written job descriptions that almost seemed designed to take the newness, conflict, and challenge out of the job.'

Job dimensions and their effects

1 *Skill variety* The way a job demands a variety of different activities that involve using a number of different skills and talents.

2 *Task identity* The way a job requires the job holder to complete a whole and coherent piece of work having a tangible outcome.

3 *Task significance* The way a job has an impact on the lives or work of other people, inside the organization or outside.

These give meaning to the work people do.

4 *Autonomy* The way a job holder enjoys freedom from supervision, independence and discretion in deciding how the job should be done.

This gives responsibility to job holders

5 *Feedback* The way the job holder receives clear and direct information about his effectiveness.

This gives the job holder knowledge of results.

Ways of getting good results on the five job dimensions

ACTION	JOB DIMENSION Affected
a *Forming natural work units* so that the work to be done has a logic and makes sense to the job holder.	2,3
b *Combining tasks* so that a number of natural work units may be put together to make a bigger and more coherent job.	1,2
c *Establishing links with clients* so that the job holder has contact with the people using the service or product the job holder is supplying.	1,4,5
d *Vertical loading* so that job holders take on more of the management of their jobs in deciding what to do, organizing their own time, solving their own problems and controlling their own costs.	4
e *Opening feedback channels* so that job holders can discover more about how they are doing and whether their performance is improving or deteriorating.	5

Material on this page is based on the work of J R Hackman, Work Design *op cit*

Exercises

1 Consider the job you now hold and think of ways in which it could be redesigned in terms of the five job dimensions listed earlier.

 a Which of those changes would *adversely* affect the work of someone else?
 b Which of the changes would *adversely* affect organizational efficiency?
 c Can those adverse effects be mitigated, or are there different changes to make that will avoid them?
 d What is stopping you from initiating the changes?
 e How and when are you going to tackle the problems that prevent you from redesigning your job?

2 Draw up an organization chart or network of the kind of business you have always wanted to set up, concentrating on how the work to be done would be divided up into jobs rather than concentrating on reporting relationships.

 a How would you alter those jobs in line with the five job dimensions?
 b How many jobs have you lost/added?
 c Will your wage/salary bill be higher or lower?
 d Would you enjoy running the business more or less as a result of the changes?
 e Are you more or less likely to gamble your life savings by starting up the business?

Further reading

SMITH J M and ROBERTSON I T. *Motivation and Job Design*. London, IPM, 1985
HACKMAN J R. 'Work Design' in STEERS R M and PORTER L W (eds). *Motivation and Work Behaviour*. 2nd ed. Maidenhead, Berks., McGraw-Hill, 1979
BRAVERMAN H. *Labor and Monopoly Capitalism*. New York, Monthly Review Press, 1974

And finally . . .

'Work banishes the three great evils of boredom, vice and poverty'
Voltaire, *Candide*, 1738

24 Understanding other people

We all need to understand other people so we can make friends, understand our families and influence others. The last of these is one of the main tasks of management, to influence other people to do things they would not do otherwise. This persuasion can be through coercion or eliciting willing cooperation. By understanding more about how other people view things, what interests them, what they see as important, the more likely we are to choose appropriate ways of influencing their behaviours towards our preferred outcome. This may be by overt manipulation of the reward system, ensuring rapport is such that the other person's view is thoroughly explored, finding something for them in what you require, or selecting the argument that the other person will find most convincing. The aim is for the interests of both parties to be sufficiently well served for there to be mutual satisfaction. To do this we need to understand how things look from the other person's view. However, seeing things from the other's view is extremely difficult. This can be helped by understanding more about the nature of individual differences and so increasing our effectiveness when working with a variety of people.

The variety of the human race is due to each of us having a unique combination of genes and experiences; even identical twins have a different set of experiences. These different combinations give us our individual ways of behaving and thinking that we call our personality. Philosophers, theologians, psychologists and others argue over the relative influence of 'nature', genes, 'nurture' and upbringing, on our personality. Some, like Freud, argue that we have deep-seated irrational and impulsive instincts, modified by acquired moral values. Others, such as Skinner, emphasize that our current behaviour is learned by experience and that we are more likely to repeat behaviours that have been rewarded in the past. There is no agreement on which explanation is correct and this has led to various models of people being developed.

Each of us operates with assumptions about why people do particular things. By making these assumptions explicit, and realizing that we work with a particular model, we will find it easier to understand that other people may be operating with an entirely different view. An important part of any model of people is to ask why do they do things, or what needs are they satisfying by their actions. We all assume that behaviour is to some extent controlled and not random. We believe that people are seeking, consciously or not, to attain certain goals.

We can look at different models of human beings and theories of motivation to help us understand customers, suppliers, other managers, subordinates or the boss. Each theory is partially accurate but only partly explains the mysteries and complexities of human behaviour. The day we can wholly account for individual variations is the day our behaviour will become as predictable as that of robots. This may make management more efficient but will be far less fun for human beings.

Management models of people

McGregor and Schein have both looked at the models used by managers. If we know what model we are using we are more likely to recognize when someone is using a different one and so make disagreements easier to unravel. McGregor distinguishes between two ways managers behave and the assumptions behind the behaviour. Schein's categories are almost a history of management thought, with the last of his categories representing the most recent view of why people will work.

McGregor described two models that managers assumed about those working for them.

Theory X managers believe:
1   People dislike work and avoid it where possible;
2   People need to be coerced to make an adequate effort;
3   People want security not responsibility.

Theory Y managers believe:
1   Effort is as natural as rest;
2   People will use self control if they are committed to the goals;
3   People seek responsibility;
4   Creativity is widely distributed in the population.

Schein describes four models managers use.

Rational-economic assumes that people are motivated by a rational assessment of their economic requirements.

Social assumes that people are seeking rewarding relationships at work and the group is more influential than management.

Self-actualizing assumes that people want, and can be, independent and responsible for their own work.

Complex assumes that there are a variety of complex desires not all of which can be met at work.

Motivation theories

Maslow grouped needs into five stages and contended that only when the needs in the lower stages were satisfied did the next stage become potent. Once a need was satisfied it was no longer a motivation although it could return later.

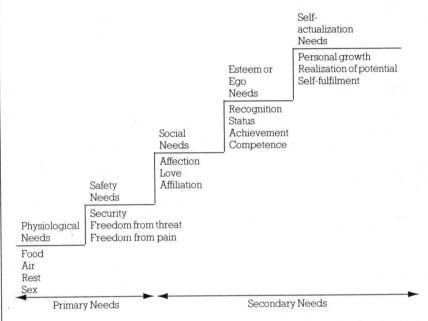

Herzberg developed this hierarchy as it effects the motivation of people at work. Hygiene factors lead to dissatisfaction if they are not up to standard but increases above this do not give more satisfaction. In contrast the satisfiers can motivate beyond the basic level as people want more of these regardless of how much they have.

Hygiene factors	Satisfiers
Company policy and administration	
Supervision	Achievement
Working conditions	Recognition
Salary	Work itself
Relationship with peers	Responsibility
Personal life	Advancement
Relationship with subordinates	Growth
Status	
Security	

It should be noted that both these writers researched amongst middle class Americans. Not everyone agrees that they can be applied across time and space universally.

Exercises

1 What criteria would you use to distinguish between understanding the needs of a fellow worker and indulging them?

2 List five factors that the interviewer is looking for in an employment interview. Now do the same thing for the interviewee. Do these two viewpoints have anything in common?

3 What assumptions do you make about those you work with? Does this fit with any of Schein's models?

Further reading

HERZBERG F. "One More Time: How do you Motivate Employees?" in *Harvard Business Review*. Jan/Feb 1968

MCGREGOR D. *The Human Side of Enterprise*. New York, McGraw-Hill, 1960

MASLOW A H. *Motivation and Personality*. New York, Harper and Row, 1954

SCHEIN E H. *Organizational Psychology*. 2nd ed, Englewood Cliffs, N.J., Prentice Hall International, 1970

ZALKIND S S and COSTELLO T W. "Perception: Some Recent Research and Implications for Administrators" in *Administrative Science Quarterly*. No 7 1962 pp 218–35

And finally . . .

Zalkind and Costello suggest the following for improving the accuracy of one's ability to understand other people.

1 The better we know ourselves, the easier it is to see others accurately.

2 One's own personality affects what one sees in others.

3 The accuracy of our understanding depends on our sensitivity to differences in people.

25 Power and authority

Power is the ability to influence others to do things they would not have done otherwise; authority is the possession of legitimate power. Power does not exist on its own, but as some part of a relationship. You can only have power over others if you have something they want. So power is part of a dependent relationship. It is also two faced; it is central to the process of social integration, but it divides people through the emergence and development of conflict over who has, or should have, power.

The dimensions of these power relationships can be described in various ways. Magnitude refers to the amount of power a person or group has; for example does the stock manager control all the materials others need? Distribution is whether power is widely dispersed, or concentrated in a few hands; can the materials be released by anyone in the stock office or only by the boss? Scope describes the range of activities over which the powerful has control; does the stock manager have power to control the budgets for purchasing new stock? The domain of power is the degree to which power in one power relationship extends to other relationships; the stock manager may be powerful when requests for materials are concerned but powerless when plans for future reorganizations are made.

To have authority is to have legitimate power, unless one takes the most nihilistic or anarchistic view that no power can be legitimate. This process of legitimizing is one of the features that distinguishes organizations from mobs. We can distinguish two types of authority; to be in authority or to be an authority. In authority is the position or title which permits the holder to have power over others. Carter (1979) discusses how this authority is dependent on other sources of power, for example control of resources, to maintain itself. Being an authority is having the skill, knowledge and expertize that others consult without compulsion. The surprise is that more managers do not try to develop an expertize of their own, as the basis of their authority, to support their positions of power.

The use of power and authority in organizations is the political action discussed in chapter 13. Whether this political action is seen as useful or disruptive will depend on the ends it is seeking to achieve. Where objectives have been agreed with others, that is organizationally sanctioned, the use of power and authority is usually seen as appropriate. Where the power and authority is used to achieve other objectives it is disruptive and inappropriate to the organization (see figure overleaf).

Sources of power

1 *Resources*
Control of what others need whether subordinates, peers or superiors.
It includes the following:
Materials
Information
Rewards
Finance
Time
Staff

2 *Skill*
Being an expert; having a skill others need or desire

3 *Motivation*
Some seek power more enthusiastically than others

4 *Debts*
Having others under obligation for past favours

5 *Physical prowess*
Being bigger or stronger than opponent; not overtly used in management except as control of resources. However, statistically leaders
tend to be taller than the led.

6 *Persuasion skills*
Bargaining and personal skills that enable one to make the most of
one's other powers, such as resources.

7 *Control of agenda*
Coalition and other techniques for managing how the issues are, or are
not, presented.

8 *Dependence*
Where one side depends on the other for willing cooperation the
power of removal exists. Strikes, or threatening to resign *en bloc*, are
two examples.

9 *Charismatic*
Very rare indeed. Much discussed in management circles as part of
leadership qualities. Usually control of resources can account for
claims of charismatic power, as many ex-managing directors have
found.

See also chapter 13.

The relationship between ends and means of power in organizations

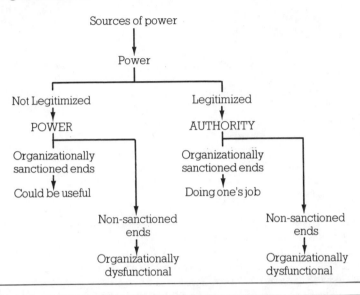

Signs of authority in organizations

Being *in* authority	Being **an** authority
Job title	Being referred to as 'our Mr/Ms ...'
Position in hierarchy	Having one's advice genuinely sought for its value, not just as a formality
Being the necessary signatory for expense claims and similar authorizations	Being able to work with considerable latitude for independent decision-making
Being a person to whom people other than direct subordinates report	Having confidence in what one is doing; not needing constant reassurance or guidance
Chairing meetings or committees	

Lord Acton, a nineteenth century historian, made a famous but often misquoted remark, 'Power tends to corrupt, and absolute power corrupts absolutely.' This is, however, only half true. Power also makes possible great achievement and can ennoble its possessor. Lord Acton's next sentence was 'Great men are almost always bad men.' Remember the words 'almost always' and make sure that your greatness produces the unusual result.

Exercises

1 Think of examples for each of the four outcomes in the figure.

2 Is it possible that the final outcome of authority used for non-sanctioned ends could be organizationally functional?

3 Which sources of power do the following have? They may have more than one.

The Queen; The Prime Minister; the leader of the National Union of Mineworkers; Steven Spielberg; Mick Jagger; the admissions tutor to a university department; your boss; yourself

Further reading

CARTER A. *Authority and Democracy*. London, Routledge and Kegan Paul, 1979

DAHL R A. "Power" in *International Encyclopedia of the Social Sciences*. Vol 12. pp 405–15. London, MacMillan, 1968

DUVERGER M. *The Study of Politics*. London, Nelson, 1972

MACHIAVELLI N. *The Prince*. Harmondsworth, Middx., Penguin, 1981

PFEFFER J. *Power in Organisations*. London, Pitman, 1981

SNOW C P. *The Corridors of Power*. Harmondsworth, Middx., Penguin, 1963

SNOW C P. *The Masters*. Harmondsworth, Middx., Penguin, 1963

And finally . . .

The only purpose for which power can be rightly exercised over any member of a civilised community, against his will, is to prevent harm to others. His own good, either physical or moral, is not a sufficient warrant.

J S Mill, *On Liberty*, 1859

26 Procedures for mutual control

Chapter 32 considers procedures for administrative action, which are the administrative drills and routines to get things done in a consistent way, without action having to be thought out from scratch every time an incident recurs.

In this chapter we look at a different application of the procedural idea, whereby two parties use procedure as a device for limiting the actions of each other. These are most common between employers and trade unions, but are also found in relationships between employers and individual employees, suppliers and purchasers and various other ways in which people work together despite differing objectives.

The main example is the procedure for the avoidance of disputes, in which an employer and a recognized trade union enshrine an agreement they have made about the action each will take in specified situations. A typical example of this is the desire of the employer to change an existing working practice. The employer may try to do this in the belief that it will improve productive efficiency, but the benefits would be nullified should the employees refuse to cooperate, or if the cooperation was grudgingly given only after protracted industrial action. The union needs to protect its members against possible exploitation and therefore wants to examine management proposals before they are introduced in order either to resist them or to modify them. As both parties are dependent on each other, they have an agreement on the procedure to be followed before the introduction of any change, with the objective of avoiding disruption.

The main example at an individual level is the grievance and disciplinary procedure, which specifies what series of steps an employer should take before attempting to dismiss an employee, and also specifies how individual employees should set about seeking a redress of grievance about their employment. Although these procedures are often negotiated by union officials, they do not depend on collective representation for their operation.

Other types of mutual control procedures deal with matters such as redundancy, health and safety, consultation and changing pay rates.

The method of mutual control procedures should follow a series of specified steps: step A is followed by step B, which is followed by step C, and so on. The steps usually involve the matter being considered by a fresh mind, eg supervisor → plant manager → general manager. It is important that the steps are few enough to prevent procrastination, but also sufficient to deploy genuinely different opportunities of resolving the difficulty. The method should then link the steps to times, so that each should be completed within a given period. The third general feature is the status quo, which will specify usually that threatened action, like dismissal, lock out, redundancy or strike, will not take place until the procedure is exhausted.

Outline model of grievance procedure

1 *Statement of purpose* The purpose of this procedure is that employees of . . . employed in . . . can resolve grievances about their employment. It offers a framework for employees to seek improvement on matters about which they are dissatisfied. It is separate from the disputes procedure.

2 *Preliminary step* The dissatisfied employee discusses the complaint with an immediate superior, giving notice that he or she would like the case heard at the next stage if it has not been resolved within four working days.[1]

3 *Hearing* The dissatisfied employee puts the case to a more senior manager. This manager, to be specified, should be more detached and thus able to judge better the implications of meeting the employee's expectations.

4 *Appeal* If the employee is still not satisfied he or she can appeal within five working days of the hearing. This will be to a more senior manager, position to be specified, to a joint committee or to an external arbiter.

Outline model of disputes procedure

1 *Statement of purpose* This procedure is to deal with matters where the employees collectively, through their representatives, seek to resolve a matter that has not been resolved through grievance procedure and where there is collective endorsement.

2 *Works conference* The matter is discussed at a conference of shop stewards and management representatives.

3 *Local conference* If the matter is not resolved, it is discussed at a further conference with the members of the works conference supported by full time trade union officials and, if appropriate, more senior managers or officials of the employers' association. This meeting shall be held within 10 days.

4 *Arbitration* If there is failure to agree at the local conference the matter shall be referred to arbitration by a mutually acceptable external arbiter, whose findings will be a basis for further negotiation.

5 *Status quo* Until the procedure is completed, the matter causing the dispute will be suspended and there will be no strike, lock out or other unauthorized action as a result of the matter.

---

[1] The number of days cited in these procedures are examples only.

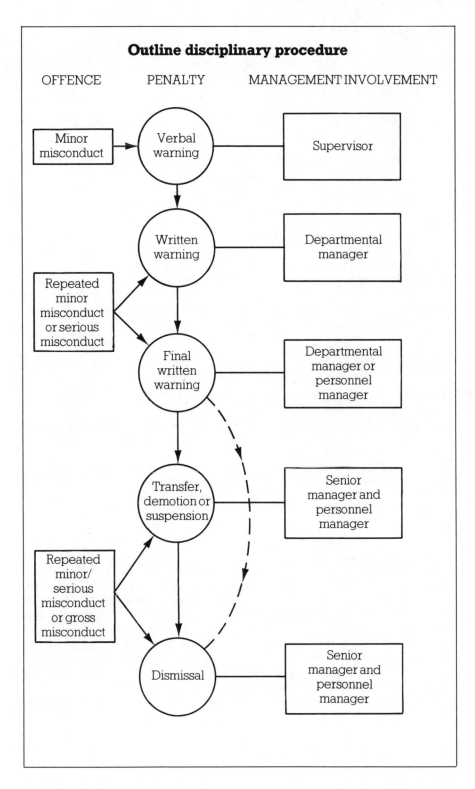

Exercises

1 Devise a promotion procedure for your organization that would ensure fair treatment for all *and* the promotion of the most appropriate without the demoralization of the others.

   a Have you made this a procedure for mutual control, or one of management unilateral decision?

   b Is this emphasis right, or do you need to make it more towards mutual control or more towards management decision?

   c What resistance would you expect to your proposals?

   d How would you overcome it?

2 What other activities in the business do you think would be improved by mutual control procedures?

3 Where are there mutual control procedures that are obsolete and which should be either abandoned or modified?

Further reading

THOMSON A W J and MURRAY V V. *Grievance Procedures*. Farnborough, Hants., Saxon House, 1976

MARSH A I and MCCARTHY W E J. *Disputes Procedures in Britain*. Research Paper No. 2 for Royal Commission on Trade Unions and Employers' Associations, London, HMSO, 1966

SINGLETON N. *Industrial Relations Procedures*. Department of Employment Manpower Paper No. 14, London, HMSO, 1975

And finally . . .

Procedures that provide effective balance through mutual control may be outnumbered by those that appear to produce balance but in fact produce imbalance. The organizational politician is tempted to negotiate a procedure which prescribes precisely what his or her opponent is to do, whilst leaving his or her own actions much more imprecise and uncertain. The opponent has little freedom of action, whilst having considerable latitude for interpretation of what should be done. In that type of situation the one with freedom of action has much greater power. However, it may be only a short term advantage as people who see themselves unreasonably constrained by procedure will soon find ways to undermine it.

Procedures, like policies, need the commitment as well as the signature of the parties.

27 Staff selection

Few managers are able to pick their own teams of staff. They have to work with the people who are there when they are appointed and may then gradually appoint one or two people to fill vacancies as they develop, or to cope with expansion. Most managers are, therefore, occasional selectors only and will be more concerned with whether or not a prospective new recruit will fit in with the established staff team, than with whether or not the person is the best equipped in other ways. Personnel specialists are more likely to steer the short-listing and preliminary interview stages, with the departmental manager coming in at the end to decide on the potential fit between appointee and existing team members.

The departmental manager can therefore assume that some form of job description will have been produced so that applicants are applying for something that they understand and feel able to do. There will also be some form of candidate specification or profile of the sort of experience, qualifications and other characteristics needed in applicants. Those two should eliminate unsuitable applicants, so that the manager is left with the question about who is more suitable than others.

For each applicant there will be an application form or curriculum vitae (CV), or both. Forms have the advantage of providing the same categories of information for each candidate in the same way, so that comparisons are easy. This is especially useful in short-listing a large number of applicants. CVs allow the candidate to choose the method of presentation and determine the content, so that there is probably more information about that particular individual.

In some organizations there will be test scores available for candidates before final selection. Managers need to guard against the temptation of interpreting these scores as 'good' or 'bad', but should take advice about their interpretation, and the weight to be placed upon them, from the personnel specialists who administered them. The use of written references appears to be slightly increasing; they have always been used extensively in the public section of employment, and their use is now slightly higher elsewhere. You need to be sure what questions have been asked of the reference writer and what is his or her knowledge of the work of the person about whom the reference is written.

You now have to interview the applicant, to decide about the potential 'fit'. The best guide for the interview will be either the application form or the CV, as both provide a structure for questioning to expand the information already pro vided. Use the interview to obtain information and develop your understanding of the candidate; leave making decisions until later. The best known guide for decision-making in selection is the seven point plan, devised by Alec Rodger. Overleaf, there is an alternative suggestion, together with suggestions about conducting the interview.

The four 'don'ts' of selection interviewing

Research has shown that the following are the most common faults of selection interviewing. Each of them can be eliminated by the person who understands the danger and uses just a little self discipline.

1 *Don't* make up your mind on the basis of first impressions and then spend the rest of the interview looking for evidence to prove you are right; you could be wrong. Use the interview to obtain information and then make up your mind.

2 *Don't* betray any tentative judgement you may have during the interview itself. Candidates will react to what they think your tentative opinions are and either try to alter them or become taciturn because they think they have failed the test.

3 *Don't* rely on the general impression the candidate gives: look for evidence relevant to the vacancy.

4 *Don't* look for reasons why the candidate will not do: look for the reasons why she or he could do the job.

Making selection decisions

J M Fraser has devised a fivefold framework for selection decisions. Use the form below to organize your thinking about candidates, marking A, B, C, D or E in each box, with A meaning much above average declining to E, signifying much below average.

	Candidates			
	1	2	3	4
Impact on others, or the kind of response a person's appearance, speech and manner calls out from others.				
Qualifications and experience, or the skill and knowledge required for different jobs				
Innate abilities, or how quickly and accurately a person's mind works				
Motivation, or the kind of work that appeals to an individual and how much effort he or she is prepared to apply to it				
Emotional adjustment, or the amount of stress involved in living and working with other people				

Conducting a selection interview

1 *Opening* Seat the candidate comfortably and then 'tune in' to each other by inconsequential discussion about the weather or a similar neutral subject. Explain what is to happen and offer plenty of smiles and nods. Relaxed candidates are more informative than terrified ones.

2 *Information exchange* Move to a more businesslike pace to obtain information and answer questions. Use a logical sequence for the interview, such as going through the stages of the working record. Use an opening question that will be easy to answer and informative, like 'Can you give me an outline of your present duties?'. Concentrate on enabling the candidate to be frank and informative. Check key points from the application form that need clarifying.

3 *Listen to the candidate* at all times; make notes; control the interview.

4 *Closing* Explain what happens next. Check that the candidate has no more questions.

5 *Review job and candidate information* Read through: job description, candidate specification, application form, interview notes, references (if any) and test scores (if any). Decide whether or not the candidate fits the job and the implications of any poor fitting.

6 *Decide between candidates* Complete a fivefold grading form (see opposite) for all candidates who fit the job. Consider how each would fit the relevant working group. Guard against unlawful discrimination. Decide to whom the offer should be made and on what terms.

References

References, especially character references, are notoriously unreliable. When reading them, remember:

1 Look for the substantive and explicit comments.

2 Do not 'read between the lines' as you may see a message that is not there.

3 Look for the recommendation. There are a number of much-used phrases, such as 'I recommend without hesitation. . .'
'I recommend for serious consideration . . .'
'Well worth considering . . .'
'Ready in many ways for promotion . . .'.

Exercises

1 Write a reference for an anonymous person applying for your job, without making it over-enthusiastic or damning. Then show it to a friend and ask if he or she would be likely to employ the person or not, with reasons. What does this tell you about the use of references? How will you modify your reading, and writing, of references in the future?

2 Use the form on the previous page to make a decision about a position contested by four candidates? Use a job and people you know, like four members of the cabinet who might aspire to be prime minister, or four of your subordinates who might be interested in your job. Is the answer you produce by this method different from your initial snap judgement or assumption? What has caused the difference?

4 Use the interview guide on the previous page to give someone interview practice, perhaps a son or daughter.

Further reading

FRASER J M. *Employment Interviewing*. 5th edition, London, Macdonald & Evans, 1978

RODGER A. *The Seven Point Plan*. Paper No. 1, London, National Institute of Industrial Psychology, 1952

TORRINGTON D P. *Face to Face in Management*. London, Prentice Hall, 1983

TORRINGTON D P and WEIGHTMAN J B. *The Business of Management*. London, Prentice Hall, 1985, chapter 12

And finally . . .

Information gathering in the interview:

'All of this has to be done in a framework and atmosphere that is not a sceptical cross-examination of an evasive witness, but a meeting in which the candidate is *enabled* (not just allowed) to talk about himself fully, frankly and with relevance to the vacant post for which he is being considered. As long as the selector organises and leads the interview, that sort of information flow from the candidate will be much more useful and informative than if the candidate is required only to provide clipped replies to a list of pre-determined questions.'

Torrington and Weightman, *The Business of Management, op cit, p 177*

28 Counselling and coaching

Counselling is not the same as giving advice and coaching is not the same as training; they are complementary aspects of the management art, which develop skill and effectiveness in another person by *not* telling him or her what to do, but by enabling him or her to find solutions to problems and to develop strengths in job performance. Both are typically provided informally and spontaneously as people talk things through and find their way past difficulties by bouncing them off another person, who provides a different perspective, so that the person with the problem develops a more rounded understanding.

Occasionally counselling is done on a more formal basis, as for instance when a graduate trainee seeks an interview with the management development officer to ask 'where am I going?' when early hopes do not seem to have been fulfilled. A specialized form is redundancy counselling, where those facing redundancy are offered assistance by the employer or by a specialized consultant. In both cases the counsel will be sought on the basis that the counsellor has some information or advice to give, but the interview would be ill founded if it did not develop as a session in which those being counselled find their own solutions, and exercise their own responsibility.

Counselling has some common features with the situations of dealing with the poor performer and performance appraisal, which are covered in the next two chapters. The similarity is that neither the counsellor nor the other person know 'the answer' before the interview begins; it is developed by the process of interaction itself.

Coaching is the art of trying to improve the performance of someone who is already competent; training is the skill of bringing someone to a level of competence in the first place. This requires a different type of working relationship, as the coach may not be a better performer, but will have elements of expertize, wisdom and judgement that the other person finds helpful. An example would be the international tennis professional, who will certainly be able to beat the coach in a match, but may depend on the coach to produce that calibre of performance by guidance, criticism and analysis.

Although closely associated, counselling and coaching are not the same thing:

> 'The proper object of *coaching* is to improve present performance; the proper job of *counselling* is the realization of potential. The former emphasises *doing*, the latter *becoming*.'
>
> F M Lopez, *Evaluating Employee Performance, op cit*

Both activities require authority in the counsellor, who must first be in a position to obtain relevant information. If you are uncertain about the progress of your career, you may receive great sympathy and general advice from a friend, but only someone in the management of your organization has the necessary information. Other aspects of the necessary authority are respect for the person being counselled, a familiarity with the coaching/counselling process, and an ability to take up the frame of reference of the other person, so that the matter is discussed from his or her point of view.

Modelling behaviour

In the counselling interview or discussion there is the opportunity for the counsellor to 'model' certain behaviours for the client in order to modify the client's mood. The main examples are:

1 *Calmness* to reduce agitation in the client

2 *Confidence* to reduce uncertainty and anxiety in the client

3 *Attentiveness* to increase the likelihood of the client being attentive as the interview proceeds

4 *Absence of dismay* should the client reveal information about which shame or guilt is felt

Methods of listening

Counsellors can be effective only if they can listen, which is more than allowing other people to talk and more than hearing what they say. Aspects are:

1 *Willingness* to listen by believing that the client has something to say and making sure that you have understood it, not making any assumptions before the story is complete.

2 *Time* to listen by indicating either that there is an unlimited amount of time, or at least that there is plenty, and not allowing any indication of impatience, like the furtive glance at the wristwatch.

3 *Space* to listen by ensuring that the meeting is private and free from interruption, and that counsellor and client do not have any awkward barriers between them, like desks or long distances.

4 *Attention* to what is being said, by strong focus on the client and the absence of distractions.

Stress inducers

Thomas Holmes, an American psychiatrist, has devised a scale of life incidents that produce varying levels of stress risk. The following are extracts from his list; the higher the points, the greater the risk:

Death of spouse	100	Divorce	73
Death in close family	63	Personal illness	53
Getting married	50	Being dismissed	47
Retirement	45	Pregnancy	40
Large mortgage	30	Responsibility	
Moving House	20	change at work	29

Stages in a counselling interview

Counselling interviews develop in many different ways, and counsellor style, warmth and integrity are more important than technique. Here is a useful sequence to experiment with:

1 *Factual interchange* Focus on the facts of the situation first. Ask factual questions and provide factual information, like the doctor asking about the location of the pain and other symptoms, rather than demonstrating dismay. This provides a basis for later analysis.

2 *Opinion interchange* Open the matter up for discussion by asking for the client's opinions and feelings, but not offering any criticism, nor making any decisions. Gradually, the matter is better understood by both counsellor and client.

3 *Joint problem-solving* Ask the client to analyze the situation described. The client will receive help from the counsellor in questioning and focus, but it must be the client's own analysis, with the counsellor resisting the temptation to produce answers.

4 *Decision-making* The counsellor helps to generate alternative lines of action for the client to consider and they both share in deciding what to do. Only the client can behave differently, but the counsellor may be able to help a change in behaviour by facilitation.

Mentoring

Mentoring is a form of coaching which reproduces in a modern organization the working relationship of skilled worker and apprentice by attaching a new recruit to an established member to induct, guide, coach and develop the recruit to full competence and performance.

One set of advice for mentors is:

*M*anage the relationship
*E*ncourage the protégé
*N*urture the protégé
*T*each the protégé
*O*ffer mutual respect
*R*espond to the protégé's needs

Exercises

1 Bartenders are the repository of many confidences as the maudlin unburden themselves late at night. Ask one or two bartenders, early in the evening, about their experiences with sad drunks and how they cope, then see what aspects of method they seem to have in common.

2 The next time you are involved in a conversation with someone who is agitated or upset, try modelling behaviour for them, as suggested on the previous page.

3 The next time you have a serious conversation with another person, try the methods of listening suggested on the previous page.

Further reading

LOPEZ F M. *Evaluating Employee Performance*. Public Personnel Association, Chicago, Ill., 1968
ROGERS C R. *On Becoming a Person*. Boston, Mass., Houghton Mifflin, 1971
CLUTTERBUCK D. *Everyone Needs a Mentor*. London, IPM, 1985
WRIGHT P L & TAYLOR D S. *Improving Leadership Performance*, London, Prentice Hall, 1985

And finally ...

There is always the risk that the client or protégé will become dependent on the counsellor, coach or mentor. Folklore reports that certain famous screen performers are unable to make love convincingly on film without a prior consultation with their analyst. Counselling and coaching can produce similar dependency and many coaches or counsellors find that dependency rather attractive as it boosts their own ego. This is, of course, the worst possible outcome, as the working performance has not been developed and may have been impaired.

29 Dealing with the poor performer

In formal organizations the responsibility of management is to organize the materials and work into suitable chunks, so that properly selected and trained people willingly perform well. But even the best run department will have the occasional poor performance. There may be problems with the materials, the organization of the work, inappropriate selection and training, or idiosyncratic problems. These problems of poor performance may be short or long term individual or group, a problem of quantity or quality or, *in extremis*, all of them combined. This chapter is mainly concerned with the long term individual problem, whether of quality or quantity.

Before anything can be done to improve poor performance, it is important to establish that there is a gap between required performance and actual performance. Whatever work is expected is communicated formally to members of the organization by the contract of employment, the company rule book, the job description, training manuals, standards and procedures. Expectations are communicated verbally at meetings and briefing sessions, individually and during training. There may be reasons for poor performance in any of these; they may be out of date, for example, or communicated inadequately to the employee.

To establish what actual performance has taken place there are various sources of information. Some, or all, of these need to be referred to when establishing the gap (see list overleaf). Having checked what is expected and what has been done, the question is whether there is a sufficient gap between the two to need attention.

Having decided that there is a gap between actual and required performance, it is necessary now to establish the reason for it. Personal reasons are those that arise from the employee's personal and family circumstances, and impede performance. This produces the ethical dilemma of to what extent, and for how long, the organization can allow personal problems to interfere with performance. Organizational reasons are those that provide a mismatch between the individual and the particular job, that can be dealt with either by clearer instructions or by transfer to other work. Individual reasons are those where the employee does not fit in with the particular working group or into the organization as a whole.

Having established the reason, or reasons, for the poor performance, ways of dealing with it will suggest themselves. This is best done by setting goals, together with the poor performer, for improvement, discussion of what additional resources will be provided in the way of clear instructions and training, and when the performance will be reviewed. The two previous stages of establishing the gap and finding the reasons for it are important, but only in so far as they serve the main objective of dealing with poor performance: improvement. A discussion with an employee about poor performance, whether in an appraisal, discipline or other interview, after reviewing the historical poor performance, should look to the future with an action plan.

A checklist for dealing with the poor performer

Establish the gap: Expected performance   Actual performance
                       Rules   Records
                       Communicated   Average

Reasons for the gap: Personal
                                                     Organizational
                                                     Individual

Ways of dealing with it: Set goals
                                                     Review them

Reasons for poor performance

Personal characteristics outside the organization's control

Intellectual ability	Physical ability	Family break-up
Emotional stability	Domestic circumstances	Health

Aspects of the organization that are outside the individual's control

Assignment and job	Investment in equipment	Planning or improvisation
Job changed	Physical conditions	Location and transport
Pay	Lack of training	Inappropriate training
Poor discipline	Inappropriate permissiveness	Poor management

Individual reasons arising from a mismatch with the organization

Poor understanding of the job	Inappropriate levels of confidence
Sense of fair play abused	Conflict of religious or moral values
Motivation	Group dynamics
Personality clashes within the group or with superiors	

Sources of information about the actual performance

Personal files	Unfinished work
Time sheets	Reject book
Sickness and absence records	Customer complaints
Work and record cards	Colleagues who come in contact
Others doing similar work to provide comparison	with the individual

Ways of dealing with the poor performer

The following are not given in order of execution but as starting points to assist thinking when a problem arises:

Goal setting
Jointly agree specific, reasonable goals, and a date to review the performance (see also chapters 30 and 33)

Training
Make sure you give appropriate training, preferably on the job, so there is no problem in making the connection between the training and the working situation (see also chapter 28)

Dissatisfactions
Fill the gap where appropriate; remedy particular problems such as pay or conditions.

Discipline
These range from the informal discussion through to increasingly formal procedures and punishment, ultimately including dismissal (see also chapter 26)

Reorganizing
Where the problem has arisen through difficulties with the work, materials, reporting relationships, physical arrangements being no longer adequately organized.

Management
Improve the clarity of communicating the task, monitoring systems or the expertize of a particular manager.

Outside agencies
Particularly appropriate where there are personal and family reasons.

The job
Transfer to a more appropriate job or department; redesign the job (see also chapter 23)

Peer pressure
Where an individual performance is very different from the average those working alongside will feel it inappropriate and may put pressure on the individual to change.

Exercises

1 Is the punctual, poor worker more or less likely to be reprimanded than the late, good worker at your place of employment? Is your company's procedure reasonable?

2 How would your boss establish a gap between your actual performance and what is expected of you?

3 Do those lowest in the hierarchy get blamed for poor performance more readily than managers because it is easier to establish a gap?

4 What systems are used in your place of employment to monitor quantity and quality of work?

Further reading

VIDEO ARTS. *So You Think You Can Manage?*. London, Methuen, 1984. Based on the John Cleese films, so popular on management courses, one of which, 'I'd like a word with you', is relevant to this chapter.

STEWART V & A. *Managing the Poor Performer*. Aldershot, Hants., Gower, 1982

MINER J B & BREWER J F. "The management of Ineffective Performance" in DUNNETTE M D *Handbook of Industrial and Organizational Psychology*. Chicago, Ill., Rand McNally, 1976

And finally . . .

The 'red hot stove rule' was originally advanced by the American Douglas McGregor, who likened effective discipline to the touching of a red hot stove:

a The burn is immediate, so there is no question of cause and effect.

b There was warning; the stove was red hot, and you knew what would happen if you touched it.

c It is consistent; everyone touching the stove is burned.

d It is impersonal; you get burned, not because of who you are, but because of what you have done.

30 Performance appraisal

Performance appraisal is an attempt to meet two sets of expectations; the employee's 'How am I getting on?' and the manager's 'How can I get them to do what I want?' The simple answer to both questions, 'Ask them' does not satisfy either enquiry. There is a hankering after more precision, more detail, more commitment, more certainty. Performance appraisal tries to meet the needs, but frequently falls short of both expectations, because people dodge commitment, are unable to be certain and generally avoid being tied down.

The main methods of appraisal are interviewing and either form-filling or report-writing, although sophisticated schemes use a more varied range. Interviews are for appraisers to discuss appraisees' working performance with them, to see how they could be improved, and to look forward to possible job or career developments. Form-filling and/or report writing are the ways in which appraisers both formulate their appraisal and convey it to a central person or group monitoring the scheme. The forms are intended to produce a degree of consistency between a number of different appraisers and to ensure that the appraisal is done as fairly and as fully as possible. Report-writing allows appraisers free reign to say whatever they like, with all the pitfalls of character references that were noted in chapter 27. Both face the problem that most managers begrudge the time involved in completing appraisal forms or reports, and are reluctant to commit themselves to a written judgement, that might produce an inconvenient reaction from the appraisee, who may expect promotion – or revenge.

The appraisal interview is very similar to a counselling interview: the person being appraised will be apprehensive about the outcome and may need a great deal of encouragement from the appraiser to engage in constructive discussion about his or her performance.

One of the main problems to be overcome in performance appraisal is the paperwork. Consistency and fairness involves a system, and systems always involve forms, which take time to complete. A second problem is the formality; managers often complain that it introduces an unwelcome rigidity into working relationships with subordinates. Often there is no action as a result of the appraisal. Both parties to the discussion may feel, for instance, that a specific piece of training is needed, or a spell of attachment to another part of the organization is required. It may not then prove possible for that action to take place, and the appraisee will not only resent the performance appraisal system, but will feel that her or his career progress is being jeopardized. Ill informed appraisers are those who are required to complete appraisals because of their place in the hierarchy, but who do not have sufficient up to date information about the appraisee's performance. The most widespread complaints are about the 'just above average' problem, because all schemes have some elements which relate the performance to a real or imagined norm, and most appraisals carry the explicit or implicit message that the person being appraised is just above average. This is easy for the appraiser and acceptable to the appraisee, but produces a general blandness that makes the scheme of little value.

Who should carry out the appraisal?

1 *Immediate superior* By far the most common practice is for the superior to appraise the performance of immediate subordinates. It has several of the problems mentioned on the previous page, but it reinforces conventions of responsibility and accountability.

2 *Subordinates* Logically subordinates are well placed to appraise the performance of their superiors, but it is a rare practice.

3 *Outsiders* Some schemes use the appraisal of someone out of the line of responsibility, like a management development advisor or an outside consultant, in order to screen out bias. The drawback is that this person will have no direct experience of the appraisee's working performance and will be limited to assessment on the basis of personality traits and the interview.

4 *Assessment centres* A specialized form of appraisal is to use a group of experts to assess potential through an extended series of activities over several days. This, of course, is concerned only with possible future jobs rather than the existing one.

5 *'Grandfathers'* Appraisal by immediate superiors is often checked by the superior's superior ('grandfather') before being finalized. This is intended as a check against bias or carelessness.

6 *Oneself* A number of organizations include an element of self-rating in their schemes on the basis that no-one has greater interest in, nor more knowledge about, the working performance than the person doing the job, so they begin the process by producing their own appraisal, which is either discussed with, or compared with the appraisal of someone else. This approach requires an organizational setting in which people feel secure and able to analyze their own performance.

Should the appraisee know the outcome?

If the contents of the final report are not disclosed to the person appraised, appraisers are less inhibited in their comments and more adventurous in their suggestions, but the appraisee will be suspicious about the contents and some go to extraordinary lengths to discover what the report contains.

If reports are revealed to appraisees, suspicion is allayed and they can have little doubt about what should be done to improve their performance and career prospects, but appraisers are more likely to be cautious or non-committal in their assessments.

Maier's three approaches to the appraisal interview

1 *Tell and sell* The interview is used to tell appraisees the outcome of the appraisal and persuade them of the need to improve in the ways specified.

2 *Tell and listen* The interview is again used to pass on the outcome of the appraisal, but the reactions of appraisees are carefully checked, and as a result the appraisal is possibly modified.

3 *Problem-solving* Job problems are discussed openly, much in the manner of a counselling interview, on the assumption that this will enable appraisees to improve job performance through enhanced understanding and the support from the organization subsequently provided.

The management by objectives (MbO) approach

A method of enhancing performance and focussing employee's actions is the MbO method which has been widely canvassed in the last 30 years. Personnel specialists sometimes elaborate it into a cumbersome administrative system, but the basic features are simple:

1 'Agree with me the results I am expected to achieve.'

2 'Give me an opportunity to perform.'

3 'Let me know how I am getting on.'

4 'Give me guidance and training where I need it.'

5 'Reward me according to my contribution.'

The problems are mainly bound up with the difficulty of setting appropriate objectives, such as increasing sales volume by X per cent only to find that a change in taxation or import regulations means that the objective is reached in three months instead of 12. Also there is a tendency to concentrate on objectives that can be measured with sufficient accuracy for there to be no argument about success and failure, rather than those which are beyond precise measurement, such as improving morale and teamwork. Furthermore, for the implicit contract to function well the objectives have to be met in the short term. What about long term developments?

Exercises

1 a Write notes on a *management* argument against performance appraisal.

   b Write notes on a *union or employee* argument against performance appraisal.

   c Try to satisfy both sets of arguments.

   d Are you better off with or without performance appraisal?

2 If your performance were to be appraised, which of Maier's three types of interview would you find most helpful?

3 Think back 12 months. If you had then agreed a set of objectives for the year that has just passed,

   a which objectives do you think would have been set, that would have turned out to be unrealistic because of *force majeure*?

   b which of your important achievements of recent months would not have been included because they were the result of events that could not have been foreseen?

Further reading

MAIER N R F *The Appraisal Interview: Three Basic Approaches*. La Jolla, Calif., University Associates, 1976
MACGREGOR D 'An Uneasy Look at Performance Appraisal' in *Harvard Business Review*. Vol. 35, No. 3, 1957. pp 89–94
GILL D R *Appraising Performance*. London, IPM, 1977
RANDELL G A, PACKARD P, SLATER J *Staff Appraisal*. London, IPM, 1984
DRUCKER P F *The Practice of Management*. London, Heinemann, 1955

And finally . . .

Our comments here have assumed an apprehensive appraisee and an omnipotent appraiser. If there is an organization culture that encourages self confidence, and an appraisee who knows what she or he is doing as well as being skilfull in analysis, the process of appraisal can be much more of a two-way exchange, because the appraisee will explain the ways in which a better service from management is needed in order to improve performance. This is the most constructive form of discussion, but depends on able people feeling secure in a culture that encourages candour.

31 Brainstorming

A senior UK management consultant has suggested that "in any organization and at any level in that organization, there exists a deep, untapped well of useful ideas". (Rawlinson 1980) However, the very nature of many organizations often militates against the independent, challenging and impulsive approach considered necessary for the production of creative ideas. Therefore, there has grown up a variety of structured aids to creative problem solving in organizations, accompanied by the belief that creativity can be acquired and improved through instruction and practice. One such technique is brainstorming, a name probably derived from the colloquial meaning of brainstorming indicating brainwave.

Brainstorming has been defined simply as a means of getting a large number of ideas from a group of people in a short time. The chief purpose of the activity is to produce a checklist of ideas which gives rise to a new and better solution to a specific problem. This is achieved by overcoming various barriers to creativity.

Many people have a tendency to conform to the methods and conventions expected or practised by colleagues. This may be politically astute, but it inhibits creative thought since it results in a lack of effort in challenging the obvious. There may be an assumption also that where information appears to belong together, the next stage is a foregone conclusion and requires no further thought. The result is an instinctive "yes" or "no" before ideas are given a chance to develop. Many ideas are thus buried at the initial stages of the thought process. People also have an excessive faith in reason and logic, and in rejecting this they risk either being proved wrong or made to look fools. The brainstorming session seeks to break down these barriers; to provide an occasion at which remote associations between thoughts and ideas may be invoked and explored to produce solutions which are less stereotyped and more creative than could be obtained otherwise.

It should be remembered that certain problems may not be suited to brainstorming exercises, for example those that are extremely diffuse or complex, or those requiring an extremely high level of specific technical knowledge. However, problems suited to brainstorming activities include the search for new products or markets, trouble-shooting, managerial problems and process improvements. Examples include finding uses for conductive plastic, reducing the amount of pollutants in rivers, improving the company's safety record or reducing fuel costs.

There are two modes of thought, vertical and lateral, which can be applied to such problems. Both have their place, and on the whole neither one should be used to the exclusion of the other when seeking solutions. De Bono points out that, like reverse gear on a car, creativity and lateral thinking is particularly useful when up a blind alley or when manoeuvrability is required.

Brainstorming seeks to provide a loosening of expression, language and thought. The aim is to use all ideas, however silly, impractical or preposterous they may seem, as stepping stones to further good ideas.

The brainstorming process

1 *Preparation*

Selection of a suitable topic for brainstorming and the participants in the session.

2 *Statement of the problem*

The group is given advance notice of the problem in the form of a brief description of one or two sentences. The originator of the session discusses with the group a limited amount of background information relating to the problem, thus introducing it into participants' minds.

3 *Warm-up session*

Participants are introduced to the concepts of brainstorming in a relaxed manner. Group discussion aims to identify the barriers to creative thinking and shows how they can be overcome. The actual brainstorming process is explained, together with the four rules of brainstorming: free association, elaboration, suspension of judgement, and speed. A short practice-run demonstrates how little time it takes to produce 50 to 100 ideas.

At the end of the warm-up session, the original problem is restated in as many ways as possible. For example, the problem of falling turnover could be redefined as how to beat competitors, or how to display better. All restatements are written down by the leader.

This session should be carried out even for experienced groups. Its purpose is to help participants escape from the pressures and constraints of daily life. It should also develop a lighthearted, easy-going atmosphere.

4 *Brainstorm*

The leader/scribe reads out the restatements and calls for ideas. As they flow, they are numbered and written up on a large flipchart with a large felt-tip pen. Each sheet is torn off when full and displayed elsewhere in the room. Noise and laughter should be encouraged. Ideas will flow fast at first and then fluctuate; a short pause can act as a stimulus for more ideas. The ideas may number from 150 to 600, or more. There should be no pre-set timescale for this session.

The brainstorming process, continued

5 *Wildest ideas*

When ideas really seem to have dried up, the leader closes the session by asking members to select the 'wildest ideas' from the list and turn them into something useful. This may produce yet more ideas, and also leads to the session ending on a high and light-hearted note. No attempt should be made to evaluate yet.

6 *Evaluation*

This takes place over the next few weeks/months, with the purpose of identifying the few good ideas for implementation and of demonstrating to participants that their efforts were worth while. The process involves scrutiny of the ideas, selection of possible winners, and examination against established criteria, such as cost, implementation time, feasibility. The final few are then chosen.

Criteria for selecting participants

Experience of brainstorming	Wide range, to include old and new hands
Background discipline	Widespread, to include outsiders and not just those working in the problem area
Personality	Needs people with constructive attitudes; a good mix of ages and sexes is useful
Company seniority	Wide range — the most senior is not automatically the session leader, but may assist later in the progression of ideas
Inclusion of the expert	Only one member should be categorized as an expert
Group size	Minimum six, maximum 20 (12 is a good number)
Inclusion of observers	No observers allowed, only participants

Exercises

1 Enquire from your training department whether your organization offers any courses in creativity, and put yourself down for one.

2 In the next three months undertake your own self-learning programme on creativity techniques, and brainstorming in particular.

3 Talk to your colleagues about brainstorming. Try to identify an organizational problem which might be resolved in this manner.

4 Think about your own blocks to creativity, and note down those to which you think you should pay the most attention.

5 Set aside 60 to 90 minutes for a warm up session at work, using the following problems as practice runs:

the noisy dog in the house next door; the large pile of bricks in the yard outside your office; the equipment disappearing from the drawing office.

Further reading

De BONO E *Lateral Thinking for Management*. Maidenhead, Berks., McGraw-Hill, 1971

RAWLINSON J G *Creative Thinking and Brainstorming*. Aldershot, Hants., Gower, 1981

RICKARDS T *Problem Solving Through Creative Analysis*. Epping, Essex, Gower, 1974

And finally . . .

Like any other management technique, brainstorming has to be understood and practised to be effective. Training should help to remove the mystique surrounding this method of problem-solving. It is important also that the culture of the organization is such that a positive and innovative approach to problem-solving is encouraged amongst all levels and all departments. The overriding principle behind brainstorming is that quantity in idea production leads to quality, so that perhaps one solution only might come out of many hundreds of ideas and many working hours. Such a process requires the organization's managers to exercise tolerance, patience and foresight.

D   Administrative action

In chapter 3 we distinguished the three main strands of what managers do as being either technical, managerial or administrative work. This part of the book is devoted to methods of carrying out a range of administrative duties, so that all the general understanding of roles and functions, and all the personal and social skills, discussed so far can be put into operation.

First is an account of how procedures can be developed to control operations and bring about consistent, economic implementation of decisions. This is the key element in running an efficient department. Two chapters on goal planning and decision making are then followed by a treatment of job analysis. A long established technique of the personnel specialist, this is being used ever more widely and is a useful method of clarifying many aspects of group working and integration. Critical path method and linear programming are two of the more durable and adaptable methods of the operations research specialist that can be used by managers to plan their activities, and chapter 38 provides a simple account of the options available in choosing a computer system. Chapters 40 and 41 pick up this theme again after some advice in chapter 39 about information storage and location. How did you rate your personal information retrieval after reading chapter 4? If you are one of the majority of managers who makes heavy use of a bulging briefcase and an overflowing 'current' file to store all the things you have not dealt with yet, then take careful note of the suggestions here.

Administrative action topics seldom crop up in management development courses because they lack excitement, but the company chairman who said that the basis of good management was getting the stamps on the letters and the letters in the pillar box was at least partly right. Which of your colleagues do you most value – the brilliant or the reliable?

32 Procedures for administrative action

Procedures get things done. Splendid ideas and bold decisions will be of little value without precise and efficient procedures to translate intention into action.

There are four main benefits of procedures. First, they reduce the need for decisions in the future. When the solution to a problem has been worked out once, the procedure provides a model for dealing with the same problem when it recurs. The procedure is a recipe, and the necessary action can be taken more quickly and by more people in an identical way than if it had to be worked out afresh.

Secondly, procedures produce consistency of action. If things are always done in the same way, those who are involved become practised in their dealings. Retail outlets develop similar procedures for dealing with customers, so that a customer will frequently need to ask only one question: "Do you serve yourself or does someone serve you?" before being able to move smoothly through the purchasing routine. Employees also become accustomed to procedural drills and are able to work together swiftly and harmoniously as long as methods are unaltered.

Procedures provide a form of control for management. Managers know that the system will keep things working correctly and smoothly, so that they can turn their attention to future challenges and current problems without being distracted by constant requests for guidance and information.

There is also the benefit of freedom from supervision. Learner drivers are under constant supervision during their first lesson, but as they learn the procedures of driving, supervision becomes less overbearing. The good administrative procedure gives staff members information and authority, so that they know what to do and how to do it, with scope to interpret the rules in unexpected situations. In this way, the benefits of management control are accompanied by the advantages of individual autonomy.

The biggest problem with procedures is that they are dull, so that few managers like to invest the time needed to get them right. Other problems can be that procedures inhibit change by providing a secure and familiar routine that people are reluctant to abandon. There is sometimes a problem of duplication, where one department has a procedure for its own stage in affairs which does not coincide with that of the next department in sequence. In producing a standard way of doing things, procedure may be interpreted as the only way of doing things and bring problems of rigidity. When procedural rigidity confronts managerial enthusiasm or employee discontent, enthusiasm undermines by 'cutting through the red tape' and discontent overcomes rigidity by 'short-circuiting the system'. The procedure will then collapse or become obsolete.

Procedures are developed by applying logic to common sense and understanding. Three common methods of finding a framework are the *check list*, *modelling*, and *flow charting*.

I Checklist of procedure principles

1 What are *all* the objectives you want to achieve?

2 Which are not really needed because there is already a satisfactory method, or because procedure is not the right answer to the problem?

3 What are the starting and finishing points of the procedure?

4 What are the interim steps to be? They should be:
a as few as possible;
b as simple as possible;
c clear and logical;
d as complete as possible.

5 Pilot the procedure by trying it out in circumstances as realistic as possible.

6 Modify procedure in the light of pilot run; re-test.

7 Implement procedure and monitor effectiveness.

II Model of instruction procedure

1 Set behavioural objectives. Decide what the trainee will be able to do when the training is complete.

2 Choose training method.

3 Meet trainee to explain what has to be done, when various standards of attainment will be reached and what the benefits of success are, giving the trainee confidence in his or her ability to succeed.

4 Present task by showing the trainee what to do: first the complete task, and then the first stage which the trainee has to master.

5 Supervise practice as trainee practices each stage in turn until the appropriate standard is reached.

6 Reinforce growing competence of trainee by explaining when something is done well and showing how overall ability is being developed. Problems are also pointed out, but with the solution also shown.

7 Evaluate instruction after each trainee has finished to see if the method or procedure can be improved.

III Flow charting

This method is used for detailed and complex administrative procedures where checklists or models would not be sufficient to encompass all the variables. The standard symbols used in flow charting are:

Operation	◯	Inspection	▢
Transport	⇨	Delay	◗
	Storage	▽	

III Sample of procedure flow chart: progress of a sales order form

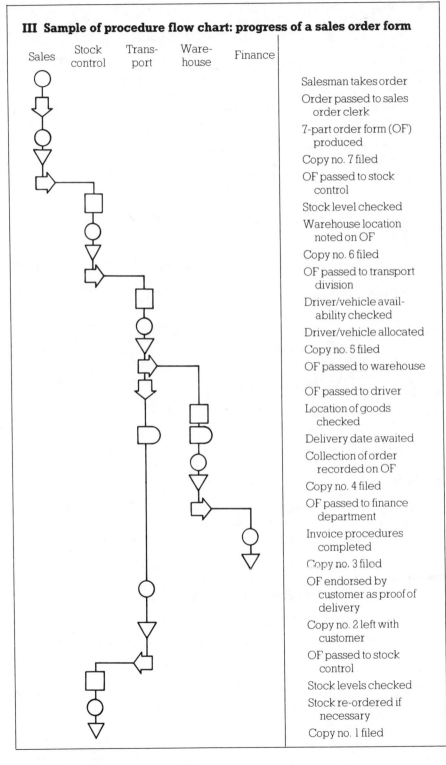

Sales	Stock control	Transport	Warehouse	Finance	

Salesman takes order

Order passed to sales order clerk

7-part order form (OF) produced

Copy no. 7 filed

OF passed to stock control

Stock level checked

Warehouse location noted on OF

Copy no. 6 filed

OF passed to transport division

Driver/vehicle availability checked

Driver/vehicle allocated

Copy no. 5 filed

OF passed to warehouse

OF passed to driver

Location of goods checked

Delivery date awaited

Collection of order recorded on OF

Copy no. 4 filed

OF passed to finance department

Invoice procedures completed

Copy no. 3 filed

OF endorsed by customer as proof of delivery

Copy no. 2 left with customer

OF passed to stock control

Stock levels checked

Stock re-ordered if necessary

Copy no. 1 filed

Exercises

1 Assume that one of the following policy decisions has been taken in your organization:

   a 10 per cent of the employees are to be made redundant;
   b product advertising is to be moved from national dailies to television;
   c numerically controlled machines are to be introduced for the first time;
   d a major new line of business is to be introduced.

Use the checklist principles on the previous page to devise a procedure to advise all those who need to know, ensuring the correct sequence of people to be informed and the necessary degree of detailed information.

2 Use the model procedure for instruction to prepare to teach someone how to carry out a series of actions successfully, such as a recipe in cookery, a conjuring trick, or wiring a plug.

3 Think of a procedure in your organization which you know well, but which you regard as unsatisfactory, and use the flow chart method to devise an improved version.

Further reading

CYERT R M and MARCH J G *A Behavioural Theory of the Firm*. Englewood Cliffs, N.J., Prentice Hall, 1963
CARTER R *Business Administration*, London, Heinemann, 1982
SINGLETON N *Industrial Relations Procedures*, London, HMSO, 1975

And finally . . .

Procedures have been described as the link between *policy* ('what we would like to happen') and *practice* ('what is happening'). Policy is a general statement of intention, like those in exercise 1 above, which has to be communicated to members of the organization, not only for them to be advised, but also for them to be convinced that the policy is appropriate. However, the policy statements also need procedures to make them work.

Policies that fail may be poor decisions or good decisions that people elsewhere in the organization never understood, but most often they are good decisions that foundered because there was no procedural follow-through.

Procedures are no substitute for policy decisions, and they are no answer to organizational problems requiring a policy solution.

33 Goal-planning and setting objectives

If managers are to lead working teams, they must know where they are heading. Thus they are constantly thinking ahead and deciding what goals to aim for, and the best means of reaching them. This is the activity of planning, but planning has a poor reputation among managers because of the frequency with which plans turn out to be inaccurate, and can hamper initiative because unplanned activities are not legitimate. There is also the danger of spending more time refining the predictions and less time on getting on with the job that has to be done, but some organization of ideas and arrangements for the future are essential to the management role.

Planning is used in various ways in management. One easy distinction is how far in the future the plans are for. Hogarth and Makridakis (1981) give a comprehensive review of the literature on forecasting and planning. Long range, or strategic forecasting and planning which looks at least two years ahead is notoriously inaccurate. This is because of difficulties in assessing the size of forecast errors, unforeseen changes in trends, discontinuities and new events and conditions. Medium term plans, for between three months and two years, are theoretically derived from long term plans, estimates of available resources, constraints and competitive considerations. The most common forms are operational budgets that act also as control mechanisms. Short term planning, for three months or less, can be reasonably accurate because of the considerable inertia in most economic and natural phenomena. Hogarth and Makridakis conclude that simple models can often be as accurate and effective as sophisticated or elaborate models. Despite these reservations planning is felt by most managers to be necessary so that they are proactive: taking initiatives and making things happen, rather than being reactive: merely responding to situations as they occur.

This chapter is about short term planning by individual managers. Goals are statements of what you are trying to do and what the priorities are. Answers to these basic questions help managers deploy resources effectively and try to help achieve neither too much nor too little. Goal planning is the process by which it is aimed to achieve the goal. It includes an assessment of the present position, how far from the goal this is, what resources are available, what will help to achieve the goal and what will hinder the achievement of the goal. Objectives are specific parts of the process that need to be met to achieve the goal. They are the detailed strategies and tasks that are the means by which the end is achieved. They are most usefully thought out in specific statements so it is clear when they are done.

Goal planning and objectives are most usefully employed when other strategies are not working. The technique is useful also where it is felt the goal will not be reached by other means, such as introducing new methods or changing old ones.

Goal planning

1 Decide what your goal is. Write it down with the criteria you will use to judge whether the goal has been met.

2 List the strengths you have already that will help you achieve the goal. Examples of the areas you might think about are given below.

3 List what you still need to reach your goal. Write these as concretely as possible so you can tell when you have met the need and it has become a strength. The same list as the strengths might help you to think about all the areas.

4 If a need is particularly difficult to achieve use the form opposite to break the need into smaller, more easily achieved objectives.

Goal

Strengths	Needs
1 Time	
2 Place	
3 Money	
4 Materials	
5 Cooperation of . . .	
6 Agreement of . . .	
7 Expertise	
8	
9	
10	

Setting objectives

1   Objectives can be to meet goals set by oneself or others.

2   Make a list of the various possible ways of achieving the goal. Asking others for their ideas may increase your list of options but they are likely to be disappointed if their idea is not used (see brainstorming for other strategies).

3   Decide which is the most appropriate method by comparing the advantages and disadvantages of each.

4   The goal-planning forms can be used to establish the strengths and needs of reaching the goal in this way.

5   When dividing the needs into specific objectives it is advisable to state them so that an answer "yes, that is done", can be given or not. Deadlines help the constantly-interrupted manager.

Need

Objective	Method	Target date	Date done
1 2 3 4 5 6			

Exercises

1 Try using the goal planning forms on something you have not quite managed to do recently. This could be something personal or at work.

2 Put the following general aims into operational form, by writing down the criteria that will determine whether or not the objectives have been achieved. If, for example, the aim was 'Get agreement on budget', this might be operationalized as "Get AB, CD and EF to agree the travel budget by 10 February". You then have three activities to undertake, and know that completing the activities will achieve the aim:

    a encourage staff to do better;
    b make more visits to customers;
    c be a better spouse;
    d monitor budget more often.

3 Turn five of the aims you have for next week into operational form. When they are completed, put dates by them.

Further reading

HOGARTH R M and MAKRIDAKIS S 'Forecasting and Planning: An Evaluation' in *Management Science*, Vol. 27, No. 2, reprinted in abbreviated form in PATON R *et al* (eds) *Organizations: Cases, Issues, Concepts*, London, Harper and Row, 1984
MACBRIEN J A *Final Report of the EDY Project to the DES*, Manchester, Manchester University Press, 1981

And finally . . .

The value of goal-planning lies in getting started. Ambitious plans sometimes fail because the planners see the ultimate objective clearly in pristine glory but are not interested in the painstaking steps needed to reach that goal. With its emphasis on the short term, goal-planning provides a means of getting through the maze of minor problems that stand between the planners and the achievement of their objective.

34 Decision-making

Some people seem to be natural decision-makers; others do their best to avoid making decisions, perhaps because they feel they should carry out more consultation, because they fear that a snap decision might indicate inflexibility, or because they want further time to adapt to the problem. However, like it or not, the characteristic of decisiveness comes high on the list of essential leadership qualities. Indecisive managers faithfully follow precedent and obey regulations but, in the words of Peter and Hull, they "lead only in the sense that the carved figurehead leads the ship". In effect, they administer rather than lead.

Managers, therefore, must make decisions whether in their capacity as facilitators, teachers, counsellors, commanders or administrators. Of course, decisions do not concern only the direction of the business. They concern also the people in the organization, the question of departmental structure and the organization of work, and the operation of systems and procedures. Many of these decisions will involve change, too often seen not as an opportunity, but as a threat. The progress of the organization depends upon such decisions being made and successfully implemented.

Most people are eager to make the right decisions: competitiveness, ambition, or the seeking of status, power and security ensures that. While success in decision-making can never be guaranteed, there is ample scope for improving our ability to avoid failure. Moreover, any increase in the number of correct decisions made can only have a positive effect upon the organization's productivity and success. While many managers may not wish to see the imposition of a totally authoritarian style of management as advocated and practised by Michael Edwardes (*see* the And finally section of this chapter), there is much they can do to sharpen up their own decision-making abilities.

Most decisions require the manager to come to terms with uncertainty. The manager has to learn to recognize the existence of uncertainty, to cope with it, to eliminate it wherever possible, and to live with it efficiently when not possible. The most senior of executives with the greatest amount of information and insight is not protected against uncertainty, since decisions concern the future, and only the past is certain. There is, of course, a difference between a good decision and a good outcome. Luck, or some other such unforeseeable event, may turn a good decision into a bad outcome, or *vice versa*. Hindsight may well make managers wiser, but they should remember that the best insurance against a bad outcome is a good decision in the first place.

Any decision involves making a choice between alternatives, and is accompanied by the attendant risk regarding the consequences of any action. Avoiding making a decision does not eliminate this risk, it merely ignores it. The choice between the various alternatives suggested in the course of the problem-solving process (*see* chapter 8) must somehow be made. The decision-maker must weight up the costs of each alternative against the benefits by selecting a solution that gives the highest/best possible pay-off for the lowest possible investment. Information is thus an essential decision-making tool. Wrong decisions are often made, not due to stupidity, carelessness or ignorance, but due to the way information is handled.

Decision aids

1 *The Checklist*

A list is made of all the factors which might be important to, or have an influence, upon the decision. The problem is thus given shape, and potentially important dimensions are highlighted. Checklists may be made more sophisticated by ascribing relative values to the different factors: for example, is return on investment more important than market size and if so, how much more important?

In selecting a research project, checklist headings might include: corporate objectives, marketing criteria, research criteria, financial criteria, production constraints, environmental/ecological criteria.

In setting up a new products team, the checklist headings might include: team objectives, position of team within company, lines of authority, personnel criteria, success criteria, financial criteria, reward system.

2 *Computerized decision support systems*

These are systematic devices for processing data and judgments. A good decision support system coordinates data, systems and techniques, and turns them into a basis for action. It should be inter-active – manager and computer acting cooperatively, each doing tasks to which each is most suited, understandable – simple, easy to communicate with, and perceived as useful – complete on important issues, adaptive and easily updated, incapable of providing stupid answers. Many such systems are on the market.

Decision support systems may serve three functions:

- Descriptive, providing explanation and rationalizing cause/effect relationships;
- Predictive, assessing, evaluating and estimating probability;
- Prescriptive, finding optimum solutions.

3 *Organization Structure*

Make use of decision-making complexes (*see* chapter 12) where decisions may usefully be made collectively.

4 *Intuition/gut feel*

This aspect is not to be ignored, since it is frequently linked to motivation and, therefore, increased chance of success. However, it is easier to defend a decision based on rational, intelligent argument than on intuition. Intuition is *not* an adequate substitute for ignorance, but still requires accompanying knowledge and skill.

5 Decision Trees

A decision tree is a means of displaying the flow of possible courses of action in the form of a branching network. A large decision is broken up into a series of smaller decisions which can be made more easily, by examining the expected monetary gain at each decision point. The value of the decision tree is that it encourages management to lay out familiar information in a manner which leads to systematic analysis, and consequently better decisions. The squares represent points at which decisions must be made; the circles represent different possible events or results of actions which are uncontrollable.

The expected monetary yield can be worked out firstly at decision point B for years 3-10, and second at decision point A for years 1-10, by multiplying the estimated yield of each outcome by their probabilities and deducting the amount invested. There are many detailed descriptions of the method of calculation in the literature. The decision tree illustrated here indicates that the best choice at decision point A is to invest £1.5m in new machinery. Further sophistication may be added by taking into account differences in the time of future earnings by using discounting techniques.

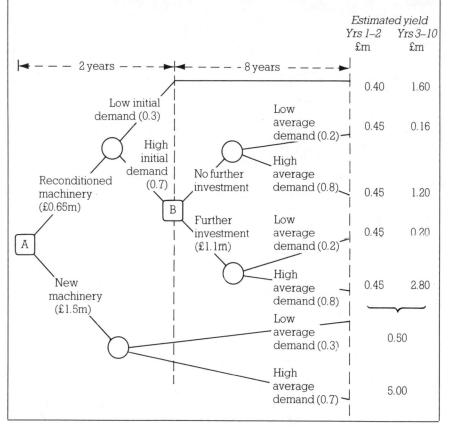

Exercises

1 What are the most important decisions you have made at work during the past three months? How long did you take over each? Do you think the use of any of the aids listed on previous pages would have improved the process?

2 Think of two examples where wrong decisions have been made in your organization in the recent past. Can you suggest why? How do you think you could do better next time?

3 Do you or your colleagues approach decision-making in a systematic and organized manner? Do you make use of any computerized decision-making aids? If not, try contacting your local software agency and talk over your decision areas with them.

Further reading

DE BONO E *Practical Thinking*. Harmondsworth, Middx., Penguin, 1971
MOORE P G and THOMAS H *The Anatomy of Decisions*. Harmondsworth, Middx., Penguin, 1976
PETER L J and HULL R *The Peter Principle*. London, Pan, 1970
SPOONER P 'UK squanders its management talent' in *Chief Executive*. November 1984 pp 10–15
MAGEE J F 'Decision Trees for Decision Making' in *Harvard Business Review*. Vol. 42, No. 4, July/August 1964. pp 126–38

And finally . . .

Michael Edwardes, in the article "UK squanders its management talent" in *Chief Executive*, November 1984, p 10–15, has blamed the weakness of management in British industry upon the lack of encouragement of individual character and personality in managers, the presence in managerial posts of individuals who lack 'inborn courage', and the reluctance of senior managers to do things that are painful or unpopular. In many cases, he claims, autocratic decision making rather than consensus is more effective.

35 Job analysis

Job analysis is the process of systematically and logically examining a job in detail to identify its components. It has long been one of the basic techniques of the personnel specialist and has an extensive range of applications.

Currently the most common use is in payment, where the analysis produces a job description which can be used to justify a pay differential between job A and job B. A second application is in recruitment and selection, where the method has been used longest. The analysis here produces a job description, so that the recruiter can then set about looking for the appropriate type of person, as well as providing summary information for the applicant. A similar application is in performance appraisal, to assist the comparison of performance with expectation. In training, analysis produces not only the job description but also the training drill or manual, so that the new recruit is taught how to perform the various components of the job. Other applications are in manpower planning, departmental staffing and sorting out problems of organization, as mentioned in chapter 12.

The standard products of job analysis are first the job description, which is a statement of the purpose, scope, responsibilities and tasks which constitute a particular job. Second is a personnel specification, which is a statement about the knowledge and skills required to meet the demands of the job description. The job description is an invariable requirement, while the personnel specification is only needed in some applications. There is always a temptation to ignore the job description and go straight to the specification: "another Pat Smith would be ideal", but what made Pat Smith ideal was as much a feature of the job as of Pat Smith.

The most common form of job analysis is the checklist, where the answers to a series of standard questions are integrated into a job description. This can be done by the job holder, by a combination of job holder and supervisor, by the supervisor, or by a specialist job analyst. Although the job holder has the most intimate knowledge of the job, he or she may not emphasize the points most relevant for the particular application. The job analyst is the most likely to be expert, but there is seldom a sufficient demand to justify such an appointment. A less popular method is the written narrative, where the job is described without the benefit or constraint of a standard format. Various forms of observation provide the most detailed analysis and the best scope for work rationalization through the techniques of work study.

There is no standard method that can be advocated, because of the range of applications. A job description to be used in selection, for instance, will emphasize job content as a means towards a personnel specification and a discriminating advertisement attracting only those likely to be successful. In payment applications, however, the emphasis is on the difference between jobs. The two applications require different approaches, as seen in the alternatives on the next two pages.

Part of a job analysis checklist for use in job evaluation

1 Job title ....

2 General statement of duties ....

3 Level of education required

    a Basic secondary   ☐   b 4–6 GCE 0 levels   ☐
    c 2 GCE A levels   ☐   d Degree in ....☐
          e Postgraduate/professional qualification   ☐

4 Amount of previous similar or related work experience necessary for a person starting this job

    a None   ☐   b Less than 3 months   ☐
    c 3 months to 1 year   ☐   d 1 to 3 years   ☐

5 How much supervision does the job require?

    a Frequent   ☐   b Several times daily   ☐
    c Occasional   ☐   d Limited   ☐
    e Little or none   ☐

6 Number of people supervised by job holder

    a None   ☐   b 1   ☐
    c 2–5   ☐   d 6–20   ☐
    e 21–50   ☐   f 51 +   ☐

7 Cost to organization of errors made by job holder

    a Under £25   ☐   b £25–£100   ☐
    c £100–£500   ☐   d £500–£5,000   ☐
    e More than £5,000   ☐

8 How often is the possibility of such errors checked?

    a Daily   ☐   b Weekly   ☐
    c Monthly   ☐   d Quarterly   ☐
    e Annually   ☐   f Not regularly checked   ☐

9 Contacts with other people, initiated by job holder

	Constantly	Often	Occasionally	Never
In own department				
In other departments				
With suppliers				
With customers				
With civic authorities				
Other				

10 Aspects of the job involving confidentiality/security

....

11 Disagreeable/dangerous aspects of job

....

12 Resourcefulness or initiative required

....

Job analysis checklist to produce job description for selection

1 Job title

2 Duties and range of responsibility

    a What has to be done
    b Relationship of job to rest of organization
    c Extent of responsibility
    d Overall purpose of the job

3 Relationships

    a Job holder reports to . . . . . .
    b Reporting to job holder are . . . . . .
    c Nature of these and other contacts

4 Physical environment

    a Where job is done
    b Hours and days of work
    c Health or accident hazards

5 Conditions of employment

    a Salary
    b Salary review arrangements
    c Pension and sick pay
    d Fringe benefits

6 Future prospects

Matrix for preparing personnel specification

Job title ....

	Essential	Desirable	Dangerous
Education and qualifications			
Knowledge and skills			
Working experience			
Disposition			
Aptitudes			
Circumstances			
Attitudes			
Age			
Car driver			
Union member			

Exercises

1 In your organization, for which of the applications mentioned in this chapter is job analysis used? Where could it be usefully introduced?

2 How can you produce job descriptions that are a useful framework for action without becoming straitjackets denying people scope or 'defensive guarantees' behind which people shelter to avoid additional demands?

3 What, if any, is the scope of using job descriptions for management control of operations?

Further reading

ROFF H E and WATSON T E. *Job Analysis*. London, IPM, 1961
UNGERSON B (ed). *Recruitment Handbook*. 3rd edition, Aldershot, Hants., Gower, 1983
ARMSTRONG M. *A Handbook of Personnel Management Practice*. 2nd edition, London, Kogan Page, 1984
HUSBAND T M. *Work Analysis and Pay Structure*. Maidenhead, Berks., McGraw-Hill, 1976

Also, all texts on personnel management have sections devoted to job analysis techniques.

And finally . . .

A useful but novel method of job descriptions is in the development of cohesion in senior management teams. The method is for the members of the team to set aside a weekend for the activity and then begin by each individually writing out personal job descriptions, according to an agreed format. Then they exchange copies with each other and study the complete set before a long, full meeting of all participants at which they pick up all the gaps and overlaps between them and find acceptable ways of dealing with those problems.

All members have to work through the parameters of their jobs and explain aspects on which others ask for clarification. The process will not only plug gaps and make sure that responsibilities fit together constructively, it will also produce a mode of working together afterwards that will probably be more effective than could be achieved by any other means, as potential gaps in responsibility between manager A and manager B have been worked on not just by those two, but by all their other colleagues as well. This results in wide-ranging understanding and appreciation.

A weekend is needed to ensure that issues are talked out thoroughly and not glossed.

36   Critical path analysis

Just as we may observe that a small percentage of the population accounts for a large percentage of the country's wealth, or that a small proportion of employees accounts for most of a company's absenteeism, it is true in many planning situations that a few occurrences will account for a large part of the total effect of the plan. An essential part of effective project planning is the positioning of the various tactical decisions within the context of the total strategic plan.

Critical path analysis, sometimes known as network analysis or PERT, enables us to pinpoint the most important of these tactical activities and thus to arrive at the critical path, which is the longest path in terms of time through the planning sequence. Now highlighted, this path can receive special attention so that the project is completed on time. Once the plan has been drawn up, progress must be monitored regularly. Deviations from expected performance levels must be reported to the foreman or other appropriate manager, who will make a forecast of the effect on the total timetable of the delay or the unexpectedly rapid progress. Any delay along the critical path will delay the whole project, since there is no slack time on this path.

To correct any slippage in a critical activity, the manager may consider transferring resources, such as labour, from other non-critical activities, or if this is not available, buying in additional resources or sub-contracting work in order to meet the project completion date. Rescheduling the work and constructing a new critical path plan may also have the effect of levelling out the use of resources and avoiding any overload which might cause delay. Although manual methods of allocating resources to networks are available, this process is normally carried out with the aid of a computer.

Critical path analysis can be used in situations where the task can be given start and finish dates; it cannot be used for continuous processes. It is applicable to projects of any size and can be carried out manually or, as previously mentioned, by computer, the latter due to the sheer number of calculations as much as to their complexity. Examples of applications of CPA include tasks such as construction and civil engineering (including all pre-contract, tendering and design work), marketing (including research, advertising and product launch) and office procedures, such as the preparation of monthly accounts. New applications are being found continually as the usefulness of the technique is discovered.

The effective use of CPA as a management tool requires understanding, commitment and care. Any failure to achieve the planned progress is firmly identified as being the responsibility of specified managers. The acceptance by supervisors and line managers of their responsibilities in such quantitative terms may not be achieved overnight. In addition, it must be understood that CPA is an aid to planning and control, not a problem solving device in itself. It is neither a preventative medicine nor a universal cure. Its chief value is that it encourages managers to set out a situation in such a way as to permit thorough examination of the problem and the effect of possible solutions and outcomes.

The three phases of critical path analysis

1 *Planning* The identification of activities and placing of jobs into their logical and correct parallel and series sequences.

Having drawn up a list of activities, the planner examines each to determine:
a what other work must be completed before the job can be started;
b what other work can be started as soon as the job is completed;
c what other work can be going on while the job is in progress.
Despite its apparent simplicity, this is perhaps the most difficult phase of CPA. It is often carried out best by a team, with a plentiful supply of paper, pencils and rubbers.

2 *Scheduling* The conversion of the plan into a feasible work schedule making the optimum use of time, labour and equipment.

From this analysis, it is possible to assign length of time to the various activities identified at the first phase and to arrive at a total time for the project. The identification of the sequence which is critical to the performance of the project, ie the critical path, is made at this stage.

3 *Controlling* The monitoring of progress against the schedule.

Actual performance can be compared with the schedule to show whether the overall project time will be achieved. A slippage in activities not on the critical path may turn out to be unimportant; a delay in the actual critical activities may necessitate action to ensure adherence to the schedule, or a reworked schedule.

The critical path diagram

The responsibility for drawing up the schedule in diagrammatic form will rest with only a few people. Copies of the diagram should be distributed, however, along with work orders, to all supervisors and it is essential that those involved in the project should know what is represented.

Sub-tasks which are necessary to complete a project are called activities and each activity is represented by an arrow to indicate whether it is consecutive or concurrent. For example:

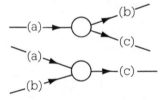

means that (a) must finish before (b) and (c) can start

means that (a) and (b) must be completed before (c) can start

Continued on next page

The critical path diagram *continued*

The point in time when a specific activity is commenced or finished is called an event, represented by a circle indicating the end of one activity and the start of another. Events are numbered in order to identify activities.

Example

If we were to take a 'simple' problem, such as buying and moving into a new house, we would identify the activities, determine their logical sequence and interdependence, assign times to each activity and then draw the critical path diagram. The result may look something like this (timings omitted):

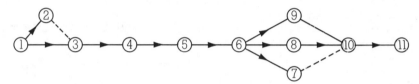

Activity

1–2	Decide the price range and type of house
1–3	Decide the area in which it is to be situated
2–3	'Dummy' activity which consumes no time and is used solely for convenience in network construction
3–4	Inspect various houses
4–5	Make and obtain acceptance of an offer
5–6	Obtain the offer of a mortgage
6–7	Apply for gas, electricity, phone services
6–8	Measure house for carpets, curtains
6–9	Exchange contracts
7–10	'Dummy' activity
8–10	Buy carpets, curtains
9–10	Complete contract
10–11	Move in

The critical path is identified only after the 'float' for each activity has been calculated. Float is spare time; the excess of available time over necessary time for each activity. The critical path is the path which has the least float. The process of calculating floats is explained in most books which examine critical path analysis in detail.

Exercises

1 Using the planning sequence detailed previously, construct a list of activities and a critical path diagram for the following tasks: painting the kitchen; launching a new product; closing down a factory.

2 Think of an example of an administrative procedure and of an operational procedure under your control. Carry out a critical path analysis on these tasks in an effort to reduce the length of time they currently take to complete.

Further reading

LANG D W *Critical Path Analysis: Techniques, Exercises and Problems.* London, English Universities Press, 1970 (Teach Yourself Books)

LOCKYER K G *An Introduction to Critical Path Analysis.* 3rd ed. London, Sir Isaac Pitman and Sons, 1969

WILD R *Production and Operations Management: Principles and Techniques.* Eastbourne, Sussex, Holt, Rinehart and Winston, 1980

And finally . . .

Critical path analysis requires goals to be set and objectives to be identified before planning can begin. In order to do this, information has to be collected from all sources likely to be engaged in the project and then fitted together logically. The symbolic representation of the project shows clearly the relationships between activities, and the interaction between participants. In this way, project and people are bound together in a flow of information-gathering and feedback that in itself will lead to better planning.

37 Linear programming

Linear programming is a mathematical tool which is used to determine the best utilization of certain resources to give a desired objective. The objective may be one of maximization of profit or output, or minimization of labour and machine costs. There will be constraints also which may limit the achievement of this objective, such as machine capacities, material availability, contractual commitments. Linear programming techniques seek an optimum solution to a problem affected by these interrelated variables and constraints.

The linear programming approach to complex problems is a major part of the field of activity known as operational research, which characteristically makes use of models to represent real situations in a more simplified form.

The types of management problems to which linear programming techniques may be applied include aspects of capacity utilization, optimum product mix and sequencing problems. All involve the allocation of resources. Their major application has in the past been in the area of manufacturing and production, but they have been applied also in areas such as planning advertising media schedules in marketing, distribution and vehicle routing, and the allocation of human resources.

Where there are only two demands competing for resources, such as two products being manufactured in one workshop, and where there is a small number of constraints on the achievement of the objective, it may take no more than the use of a piece of graph paper and a pencil to avoid a potentially damaging course of action being taken. Graphical optimization is the simplest method of linear programming. It has the advantage of showing clearly the relationship between the variables, and it can demonstrate also the effect of different courses of action to non-numerically minded colleagues, especially with the use of pins and coloured threads on a board.

However, where the factors of the problem are more complex, a graphical solution may not be feasible and solutions based on more sophisticated linear programming techniques using matrix algebra have to be used. The most common of these techniques, which consist of a large number of separate steps, is the Simplex method. These methods are highly repetitive and are thus highly suited to computerization. When a case to be considered involves 20 or 30 different products with hundreds of constraints, a solution is unlikely to be found manually, due to the tediousness of the calculations rather than their complexity, whereas a computer can carry out an examination of the possible solutions in a few minutes.

Linear programming, however, may place certain artificialities into the statement of a problem. Its principal limitation is that, being a linear approach, requirements and costs are proportional to quantity. For example, it assumes that if one tonne of steel costs £1,000, then five tonnes will cost £5,000 with no discount. Such directly proportionate relationships, however, are often a helpful simplification of real life and the results obtained are usually more satisfactory than a rule of thumb approach.

Graphical solution to a linear programming problem

A factory workshop produces two qualities of carpet underlay. The 'standard' quality requires 1.5 hours on process A and 1 hour on process B, and the 'deluxe' quality requires 2 hours on process A and 3 hours on process B per production length. The difference between the cost of raw materials and the selling price per production length is £20 for standard and £30 for deluxe. It has been agreed with the unions that each process cannot be operated for more than 2,400 hours with current staffing levels. All output of deluxe can be sold, but it is decided that production of standard underlay should not exceed 1,200 lengths.

How many lengths of each quality of underlay should be produced in order to maximize gross profits of the workshop?

1 Present the problem in tabular form, as follows:

	Hours required per production length		Total hours available
	standard (S)	deluxe (D)	
Process A	1.5	2	2400
Process B	1	3	2400
Profit per length	£20	£30	
Output requirements (lengths)	0–1200	0 or more	

2 Set the parameters of the model, as follows:

a 2,400 hours are available to provide 1.5 hours for each unit of S produced and 2 hours for each unit of D, using process A.

b 2,400 hours are available to provide 1 hour for each unit of S produced and 3 hours for each unit of D, using process B.

c The output of lengths of S is limited to 1,200 or less and, since production cannot be negative, both S and D must be at least zero.

d The objective is to obtain as large a contribution (C) as possible, based on contribution levels for each quality of product of £20 for S and £30 for D.

The model can be expressed like this:

$$\text{Maximize } C = 20S + 30D$$
$$\text{When} \quad 1.5S + 2D \leqslant 2400$$
$$\text{and} \quad S + 3D \leqslant 2400$$
$$\text{Subject to the limits } S \leqslant 1200$$
$$\text{and } D \geqslant 0 \leqslant S$$

3   Take each constraint and change it into a linear equation, then plot this straight line on a graph. (eg 1.5S + 2D ≤ 2400 becomes 1.5S + 2D = 2400, and is a straight line running from S=0, D=1200 to D=0, S=1600)
When all the constraints are plotted, the graph should look like this:

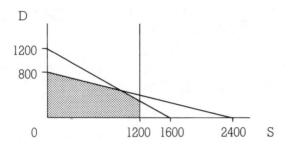

The solution lies within the 'feasibility area' bounded by the three constraints, represented by the shaded area.

4   Draw a line for the function C = 20S + 30D, starting at say C = 12000, and move it outwards from the origin 0 in a series of parallel lines until it touches only the outermost corner of the 'feasibility area'. Contribution is at its maximum at this point.

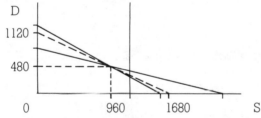

This point can be located graphically to show that the optimum mix is to make 960 lengths of standard underlay and 480 lengths of deluxe underlay. This will bring in a contribution of £33,600 (since C = 20S + 30D, and where S = 0, D = 1120, and where D = 0, S = 1680, then C = 30D or 20S).

Exercises

1 Discuss with colleagues two examples where the ideas of linear programming could be applied in practice in your organization.

2 Carry out the following exercise in maximization by graphical representation:

A company manufactures two products, bedside tables and bookshelves, from two materials, hardboard and veneered chipboard. There are 300 kilos of chipboard and 210 kilos of hardboard available. Each bedside table requires 4 kilos of chipboard and 2 kilos of of hardboard, whilst a bookshelf requires 3 kilos of each material. The profit per unit is £5 for bedside tables and £4 for bookshelves. What production mix will maximize the total profit?

Further reading

HARRIS J and POWELL J *Quantitative Decision Making*. Harlow, Essex, Longman, 1982

TENNANT-SMITH J *Mathematics for the Manager*. Walton-on-Thames, Surrey, Nelson, 1971

WILD R *Production and Operations Management*. Eastbourne, Sussex, Holt, Rinehart & Winston, 1980

YEOMANS K A *Applied Statistics*. Harmondsworth, Middx., Penguin, 1968

And finally . . .

Linear programming, as with all operational research methods, involves the following steps: recognise the problem; define the problem; represent model of the situation; manipulate the model; select the optimum solution; implement the solution.

The first two steps are often the most difficult. However, they are also the most vital, since an incorrect diagnosis at this stage is likely to result in an incorrect solution.

38 Computer systems

Computers are concerned with handling the masses of data involved in the multiple transactions of an organization. The tasks they perform include creating and modifying data, sorting and storing information, selecting and accessing records, computation and statistical analyses, and controlling systems and machines. Whether used in the accounts office to carry out invoicing and sales order progressing, the marketing department to aid with sales call planning or media scheduling, the personnel department to maintain records, or as part of the manufacturing function to plan, monitor and control the flow of work, computers provide a vital information processing service.

Computers are frequently linked together to form networks which can communicate electronically with each other. A network may incorporate three classes of computer: the powerful mainframe, the mini-computer which has less processing capacity, and the user-friendly desk-top micro-computer. Such a system provides differing levels of performance and capability which benefits all areas of the organization. Minis and micros, for example, do not require an air conditioned environment and are thus suited to laboratories, factory workshops and individual offices.

The existence of a networked system means that the information in the central data processing unit can be accessed by every part of the organization, thus ensuring a consistency in the treatment of historical, current and estimated data. For example, a detailed sales breakdown may be fed into the warehouse stock control system, called up on the public relations word processor, used by the graphic designer in the publications unit, fed into the financial control system, as well as being used extensively in the marketing department.

However, a computerized system is only as good as its data. Whereas errors in manual systems can be located and isolated quickly, data in an electronic system may be used and re-used at high speed in many parts of the system, spreading errors rapidly and causing severe problems. The likelihood of this happening can be reduced, of course. Each department should be made responsible for the quality of its own data, frequent appraisals of the state of data should be undertaken, and managers and personnel should be competent and well trained to run the system.

The introduction of sophisticated electronic processes into an organization may be met with resistance, especially from those whose jobs or skills they make redundant. It necessitates the presence of a cultural climate that encourages the acceptance of change, for example by explaining changes before they occur to all staff, being tolerant of initial mistakes and involving people in the whole process.

It is vital also that organizations choose and develop the appropriate systems in the first place. ICL describe the 'right' system as "that which will deliver the greatest improvements in productivity possible for the investment being made, and which will protect that investment against obsolescence in the future". These criteria can be satisfied if a system is chosen which accurately reflects: the exact nature of the tasks to be performed; the size of those tasks; the quantity of information to be accessed and transferred between departments and offices; the degree of planning flexibility required in terms of whole system now or extend in the future as necessary; and the available budget in relation to potential savings in costs and higher productivity to be gained.

Computer network in a manufacturing organization

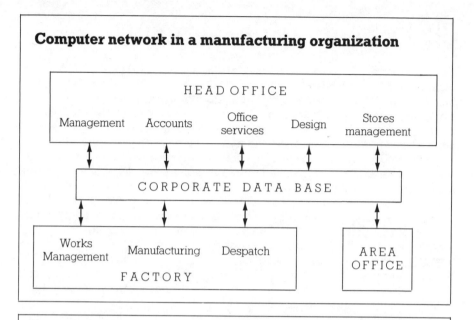

Specialist terminals

These can be supported by a mini-computer, or may be connected to a mainframe computer via a mini-computer as part of a network.

Type of terminal	Function	Application
Data collection	Collection of data from shop floor, office, stores, warehouse; instant update of files for planning and control purposes	Manufacturing, construction and maintenance, administration, all work in progress, machine utilization and shortage control activities
Option selection	Provision of fast and informed response to enquiries and orders by staff in direct customer contact; provision of alternative options to guide operator and customer towards correct transaction	Sales, retail outlets, stores, warehouses, stock control, telephone selling departments, wholesalers
Time and attendance	Collection of attendance times, passage of data to payroll	Multiple entry points: large works/sites with many employees
Retail terminals	Cash/credit transactions at point of sale, including in-store data collection	Retail operations: department stores, food stores

Types of data-processing systems

Periodic processing
(file processing
systems closely
resembling manual
methods of DP)

Large volumes of data of identical type where batches of data are processed from time to time in one operation.
EXAMPLE: Payroll

Real time systems
(no manual
counterpart)

Small quantities of data processed in one operation, causing minimal delay.
Process control: continuous monitoring and controlling of operational processes, with rapid processing of data.
EXAMPLE: Oil refining, monitoring/control of pressures, temperatures and composition of substances
Information storage/retrieval: access and updating of data in small quantities, necessitating minimal calculations.
EXAMPLE: Hospital records system
Transaction processing: handling specifically defined transactions one at a time; small amount of data; processing may include calculations and updating.
EXAMPLE: Airline seat reservations

Database systems

One store of information to support all the data processing activities of one company; independent of any individual application.

Programming languages

FORTRAN   (Formal Translation)
Scientific and engineering applications

ALGOL   (Algorithmic Language)
General purpose, but oriented towards scientific and engineering areas

COBOL   (Common Business Orientated Language)
Commerical data processing

BASIC   (Beginners' All-purpose Symbolic Instruction Code)
General purpose and computer education

PASCAL   (Named after Blaise Pascal, inventor of first mechanical calculating device)
General purpose and computer education

PL/M   (Programming Language/Micro-processors)
Programming of microcomputers

RPG   (Report Program Generator)
Production of reports and summaries from commercial files

Exercises

1 Investigate and make yourself aware of the computer systems in your organization. Make a rough paper-and-pencil plan of the location of the processing units, the terminals and the communication links.

2 Are you responsible for any development in the computing system for your organization or are these decisions taken elsewhere? If the former, do you take positive steps to encourage a climate for change? If the latter, are you aware of, and happy about, any developments you know are in the pipeline?

3 Have computers in your company increased productivity? For whose benefit? At whose expense?

4 How much effort are you making personally to learn and develop your computer skills?

Further reading

BISHOP P *Computing Science*. Walton-on-Thames, Surrey, Nelson, 1982

INTERNATIONAL COMPUTERS LIMITED *Information Systems: An Introduction to Information Technology*. London, ICL, 1983

PUTNAM A O *Management Information Systems: Planning, Developing, Managing*. London, Pitman, 1980

And finally . . .

The recent vast expansion of 'information technology' is not the result of the existence of the computer *per se* (since digital computers have been around since the mid 1940s), but rather of the reduction in the cost of computing power due to the mass production of the silicon chip. However, we may drive cars manufactured by robots, do our shopping by electronic funds transfer, fly in planes and be operated on by personnel trained in simulators but, despite the 'IT revolution', we are unlikely to be working in the paperless office for many years to come.

39 Information storage and location

A business has five critical resources: money, materials, machines, people, and information. To manage the future of a business is to manage all these resources. The efficient use of information depends on the way it is organized. Information is different from data: data are quantitative or numeric notions which need to be coded, interpreted or processed in order to become qualitative concepts and ideas forming the basis of information.

The process of obtaining, selecting and examining information for any one particular task can be onerous, but in this respect computers have provided a large capability for information storage and location. Technological advances have opened up new opportunities for better control, by reducing data processing costs and increasing the speed of information handling. Functions such as statistical forecasting, order handling, design, accounting, stock control, distribution, production scheduling and materials handling have all been made easier through the use of automated information and control systems. In addition, electronic data processing has the potential to reduce the amount of routine clerical labour involved in the handling of information.

Management consultant Arthur Putnam suggests that a successful business information system requires an accompanying philosophy which regards the system as the "nervous and response system" of the organization. Such a system must be designed and developed to be the servant of the organization's managers and therefore managers should be encouraged to participate in the design and operation of the system they need. The successful business information system operates across departmental boundaries and it is essential that the system receives attention and commitment from top management.

Feeding into the organization's own information system is knowledge gathered by many external bodies. Electronic libraries can provide information worldwide on such subjects as patents, medical and chemical products and the law, using sophisticated techniques to search through the wealth of technical literature available. Their use, for example, may enable an obscure legal judgement to be accessed in 15 seconds instead of in four days. Such information may be regarded as a product, and public access to it has to be bought. This applies also to the many communication links which exist for the passage of information: videotex systems such as Prestel which link computer information to the television set; electronic mailboxes such as British Telecom Gold which provide distant offices with computerized messaging services; and automatic indexing/abstracting services which enable information from newspapers and journals on specific topics to be identified and passed to subscribers.

The manager whose office information system consists of filing cabinets and a word processor also has the ability to maximize its efficient use. As with any information storage system, attention should be given to the quantity of information, the importance of speed of access, the uses for which it is required, and the ease of updating. Merely being aware of the important role of information will help managers strengthen their information handling techniques.

The flow of information

Risk handling = handling of uncertainty = *information handling*

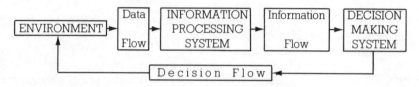

The handling of information involves the following:

- the *acquisition* of information; (concerning results, opportunities etc.) via formal/informal channels; by active/passive means

- The *processing* of information: storage; use; memorization

- The *transmission* of information: regular/*ad hoc*; written/word of mouth; upwards/downwards

Help yourself in the management of information

1 Know the key people: know and establish contact with the major contributors in the field, and study their work. Know the political controllers of the flow of information.

2 Know the key sources: of the acreage of information available in your field, a few sources will probably cover most of your needs.

3 Have an efficient alerting system, to cover significant items of information you may otherwise miss yourself.

4 Do not keep it. Too much material is a deterrent to an efficient information system. Rely on external information services and keep only a few specific items yourself.

Adapted from Holm, *How to Manage your Information, op. cit.*

Organizational information analysis

Type	*Area*		*Subject*
EXTERNAL (ie factors largely outside company control)	i	The environment	Suppliers of the factors of production (raw materials, labour, money), Government, Law, the media, consumer associations, social trends and demographics, etc.
	ii	The market	Size, trends, structure; Competition
INTERNAL (ie factors inside company control)	i	The organization	Strengths and weaknesses; the trappings and the substance
	ii	The products or services	Range, life cycles, balance of growing/declining products

The above has particular reference to a marketing information system but can be adapted for other areas of the business.

The work station of the future?

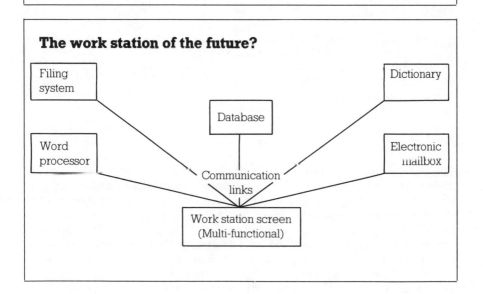

Exercises

1 Carry out a quick analysis of the information system in your organization with respect to the following:

Does the information it provides satisfy your own needs?

Does it enable you to have access when and where you want?

How would the loss of information affect you?

Is the information based upon data of sufficient accuracy and in a form that can be readily interpreted?

Is it easily updated, by you and by others?

2 If the above analysis shows up some deficiencies in your information system, note down ways in which it could be improved.

3 What is your understanding of the practical operation of the flow of information in your organization/department. For example, do you know where the power over information is located and who the gatekeepers of information are? (Wintergreen, the HQ mailing clerk in *Catch 22*, by Joseph Heller, determined the outcome of the power battle between General Dreedle and General Peckham by throwing all communications from the latter into the wastepaper basket)

Further reading

BECKER J and HAYES R M *Information Storage and Retrieval: Tools, Elements and Theories.* New York, John Wiley, 1963

HOLM B E *How to Manage your Information.* New York, Reinhold, 1968

PUTNAM A O *Management Information Systems: Planning, Developing, Managing.* London, Pitman, 1980

And finally . . .

The handling of information via electronic rather than manual means has wide social implications including the depersonalization and deskilling of work, and the widening of the gap between the information rich and the information poor. Another aspect is that of data protection. The Data Protection Act of 1984 is intended to limit the potential for misuse of personal information processed on a computer. However, there are many exemptions in the areas of tax, crime, national security, payrolls, accounts, consumer credit and research. Paper records remain uncovered by any protection offered in the Act to computerized records.

40 Project analysis and investment appraisal

Decisions concerning the investment of funds in capital projects are not those which can be changed normally without substantial cost and therefore are not to be taken hastily. The acquisition of long term assets may affect both the profit earning capacity of the business and the nature of the organization's activities for many years to come. Given the nature of the risks, the financial stakes and the time spans involved, careful analysis is vital.

Projects to be appraised may concern the acquisition of a new warehouse, new machinery, new vehicles, a new telephone exchange or computerized information system; they may concern the implementation of advertising campaigns, energy saving programmes or repairs to property; they may concern the continuation of the organization's research and development programme. Such projects may seek to replace old equipment, to save labour costs, to increase capacity, to reorientate or diversify the business, to improve the company's position in the marketplace. Whatever the 'problem', there is likely to be a choice of possible actions (see chapter 8). With capital projects, analysis is required of all the available options in order to compare cash outflows now with cash inflows in the future and to determine if the rate of return on the investment is good enough and the project is profitable. Even when profitability as such is an inappropriate objective, eg in connection with the provision of medical/welfare facilities for staff, or measures to satisfy legal safety requirements, there is a need to utilize all resources to the best possible advantage.

Analysis techniques will help in identifying those areas in a proposal which can be quantitatively evaluated, and in focusing attention on areas where qualitative judgement needs to be exercised. Where projects are being analysed for the purpose of determining the optimum use of capital, the use of a common standard enables the comparison of schemes against each other, and quantitative appraisal techniques are therefore of considerable value. Some of these are summarized on the following pages. However, a purely rationalistic, 'black box' approach to investment decisions is often unrealistic and unhelpful. For this reason, many evaluation techniques are available which seek to combine a quantitative cost-benefit approach with a qualitative checklist approach. (Checklists are discussed in chapter 34.)

Although they do not guarantee the financial success of a project, investment appraisal techniques are a useful means of instigating the collection of information, the organization of communication between different parts of the company, and the discussion of all the factors involved. All these activities are essential requirements of the decision-making process. Appraisal techniques are aids to decision making. They provide the manager with sets of procedures which process data and judgements and which provide guidance. Managers still need to apply their own experience and discretion to the weight to attach to the qualitative/quantitative estimates, the acceptable level of risk and benefit and, perhaps most important, to whether the project is in line with the planning objectives, the goals and the policies of the organization.

Methods for analyzing project proposals

a *Non-discounting techniques*

1 Payback method

Calculates the time needed to recover the original investment by estimating the cost of the project and the amount of cash likely to flow in to the company as a result of the project

Advantages Can be used as a preliminary screening method if payback period is a criteria for acceptance; easy to calculate tends to eliminate high risk proposals; emphasizes short term conversion of assets into cash
Disadvantages Ignores long term profitability (no account taken of revenue beyond the payback period); ignores the time value of money; inadequate unless used in conjunction with other methods

2 Return on investment method

A commonly used indicator of profitability as measured by the percentage relationship of average profits over the life of the project to the original investment. Useful as a basis for assessment of overall performance

Advantages Extends the calculation over the useful life of the project; allows ranking of different proposals by a rate of return, which may then be compared with a minimum acceptable rate of return figure
Disadvantages Ignores the cost of money over time; averages out yearly fluctuations in profit; ignores the timing of cash flows

b *Discounting techniques*

1 Net present value method

Uses a selected rate of interest (cost of capital to the company, or a minimum return figure) to discount the proposal's cash flows to present values', the total of these present values is deducted from the present value of the capital outlay. If this results in a positive figure, the project is acceptable

Advantages Allows for the time value of money; includes all cash flows in the calculation; allows taxation aspects to be taken into account
Disadvantages Assumes certainty in prediction of interest rate, and amount/time of cash flows; does not relate NPV to size of investment

Continued on next page

2   Internal rate of return method
    (or yield method)

Used to identify the rate of return at which a project's discounted incomings and outgoings will balance; involves a lengthy process of trial and error, but ideally suited to computerized calculation. The return yielded is compared with the cost of capital and, if the yield exceeds the latter, the project is acceptable

Advantages . As for NPV plus: Concept of 'yield' readily understood by management; can be ascertained by interpolation or by visual presentation on a graph *Disadvantages* Multiple solutions may be reached if the cash flows are non-conventional (ie where cash inflows do not always follow cash outflows); makes assumptions about cash flows

Practical problems of appraisal

i   The preparation of estimates of inflows/outflows is time-consuming and imprecise. Assessment of demand rates, selling prices, growth rates, life of assets, yields of plants, maintenance costs and interest rates is extremely difficult. Wide margins of error are common, especially in R & D projects, or where there are no comparative projects. Errors are often not attributable to inexperience. The probability of market success or sales revenue is often harder to estimate than the probability of development costs. Innovations where the future market potential was grossly underestimated include: electronic computers, numerically controlled machine tools and robots, polythene and PVC. Those which suffered over-optimism include the fuel cell, the airship, synthetic leathers and Concorde.

ii Uncertainties often cannot be removed before the commitment of major resources is made. These uncertainties may be to do with the market, the technology or the environment. The handling of risk, however, is often made easier by a high quality of information handling (*see* chapter 39).

iii Proposals and projects to be appraised are frequently inter-dependent, or have implications for other parts of the organization. The evaluation of interrelationships is highly complex.

iv Financial analyses may ignore other factors, such as labour require-ments and flexibilities, or constraints upon capital.

Exercises

When undertaking any capital investment appraisal, try to consider your own attitude towards risk and incorporate risk into the decision process. Harvey and Nettleton suggest you ask yourselves the following questions:

1 What is the qualitative 'value' of the proposal to the section/department/organization?

2 What are the range of outcomes which may arise?

3 Are any of the possible outcomes crucial to, or threatening to, survival?

4 What is top management's reaction likely to be if the proposal achieves the best, and the worst, possible result?

5 What strategies can you adopt to reduce the associated risks?

6 What is the relationship between possible returns and the levels of risk associated with the proposal?

Further reading

FREEMAN C. *The Economics of Industrial Innovation*. 2nd ed London, Frances Pinter, 1982

HARVEY D A & NETTLETON M. *Management Accounting*. London, Mitchell Beazley, 1983. (Core Business Studies)

HORNGREN C T. *Cost Accounting: A Managerial Emphasis*. 5th ed. Englewood Cliffs, NJ, Prentice Hall, 1982

ROBSON A P. *Essential Accounting for Managers*. London, Cassell, 1966

And finally . . .

Any appraisal method is useless unless the organization is prepared to devote resources to planning and research activities. In order for the right type and quality of proposals to be submitted for appraisal in the first place, there needs to be an established search system for projects which is integrated into organizational processes and administrative procedures.

41 Activity scheduling

"The first step towards understanding work", comments Drucker, "is to analyze it". Knowledge of the 'syntax' of work activities, their relationships, connections and configuration, enables management to plan, control and evaluate the steps which are being undertaken to achieve the desired end. Techniques such as objective setting, network analysis, linear programming and budgeting (all discussed in other chapters) are processes which help determine the nature of future activities of the organization by asking the question "Where do we want to be?", and then "How do we get there?". Activity scheduling is another such technique.

Functions such as purchasing, marketing, production, personnel and finance all involve activities which have to be scheduled in order to meet commitments within constraints. Achieving a satisfactory balance between the utilization of resources and the level of service offered is the principal objective of activity scheduling.

One method which provides a basis for many schedules is that of Gantt charting, named after its originator. This is a visual display of the planned order of activities over a period which allows for continuous monitoring and control while the plan is in operation. Activities are listed down one side, and the time taken by each activity is represented by a horizontal line, measured in minutes, days, weeks, or months as appropriate. To show how work is progressing, a bar or line is superimposed which represents the amount of work actually completed at stated times. Gantt chart schedules may be built up forwards with each job being scheduled as early as possible after completion of a previous job, or backwards, working back from the 'due-date' in order to determine the start date for the operation. They may be used to show the schedule of work for one particular operation from start to finish, to show the work load on one piece of equipment or machinery, to monitor progress or to display work patterns and rotas for groups of people. These charts can be highly informative, combining both the planning and recording of progress where their use has been highly developed. Gantt charts can also show the interrelationships between activities, eg a requirement that two activities must be completed before the third activity is started. This can be done by converting a network diagram (*see* chapter 37) into a Gantt format, thus highlighting milestones in the critical path, but in a chart as opposed to an arrow diagram form.

Where there are hundreds or thousands of operations to be scheduled, it may become impossible to use manually composed schedules, since the delay of one operation may require the rearrangement of many others. In these circumstances, Gantt charts may be constructed using computer programmes, taking care that a schedule produced in this manner is realistic and is attainable rather than merely 'optimum'.

Schedules should not be kept locked away in the manager's desk. As dynamic aids to planning and control, they should be openly displayed on the office wall or workshop noticeboard and continuously updated. By using a daily update system, supervisors and staff will develop confidence in the schedules and their relationship to their actual work.

Activity scheduling – aims, preparation, problems, effectiveness

Aims and objectives of scheduling

Completion of work by due-date; maximization of output; minimization of operator/machine idle time; minimization of material waiting time, minimization of costs, maintenance of even balance of work load and work flow; maintenance of balance of equipment utilization and labour utilization; provision of information on which to base realistic and reliable delivery promises

Factors to consider in the preparation of schedules

Existing commitments; available resources; machine and operator efficiency; work content of task under consideration; method and sequence of task components; maintenance commitments; holidays and training; allowances for sickness, absenteeism, reject work, machine breakdown (facilities may be loaded to 75 per cent capacity, for example, to allow for potential delay)

Problems in scheduling

Failure to identify objectives; large variety of component tasks and methods; material shortages; accuracy of data; changes to schedule

Failure of top management to understand the importance and implication of planning and control through scheduling. This results in the absence of: defined responsibilities: formation of unambiguous company policy; appropriate training and recruitment activities; non-preferential delivery promises

Failure of line management to adhere to the schedules; establish feedback mechanisms for job progress; devise systems for updating schedules and revising priorities at frequent intervals; distribute information to operating personnel

Measures of effective scheduling

Level of output; percentage resource utilization; number of clients/customers; client/customer 'queueing' time; percentage orders delivered on or before due-date; percentage shortages or stock-outs; number of complaints

Acknowledgement: B. Dale

A *Shift rota*

Team	January															
	1	2	3	4	5	6	7	8	9	10	11	12	13	14	15	16 etc
A	D	D	N	N	–	–	–	–	D	D	N	N	–	–	–	–
B	–	–	D	D	N	N	–	–	–	–	D	D	N	N	–	–
C	–	–	–	–	D	D	N	N	–	–	–	–	D	D	N	N
D	N	N	–	–	–	–	D	D	N	N	–	–	–	–	D	D

Four-shift system: each team works two 12-hour day shifts, two 12-hour night shifts, then has four days off

B *Progress chart*

Sales Programme: units sold as at week 22

	April					May					June		
Week no	14	15	16	17	18	19	20	21	22	23	24	25	26
Product A	80	80	60	80	80	80	80	80	80	80	80	80	80
B	–	–	–	–	–	40	60	60	60	60	60	60	70
C	40	40	40	40	40	40	40	40	40	40	40	40	40

The lines show progress up to the time indicated by the arrow. Product B is being sold according to plan, product A is ahead of forecast, and product C is behind schedule.

C *Work schedule*

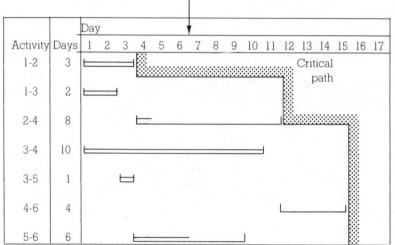

Activity 2-4 is behind plan, and lies on the critical path, so highlighting the need for urgent remedial action.

D *Load chart*

Machine no	Mon	Tues	Wed	Thurs	Fri
472					
903					
701					
703					

* represents passage of one work task through the schedule
s represents machine setting-up time

Exercises

Draw up the following activity scheduling charts:

1 Progress chart of getting ready to move house;

2 Work schedule for the summer's gardening programme;

3 Load chart for a conference.

Further reading

BURBIDGE J L. *The Principles of Production Control.* 2nd ed. London, Macdonald & Evans, 1967

DRUCKER P F. *Management: Tasks, Responsibilities, Practices.* London, Wm Heinemann, 1974

LOCKYER K G. *An Introductioin to Critical Path Analysis.* 3rd ed. London, Pitman, 1969

WILD R. *Production and Operations Management: Principles and Techniques.* Eastbourne, Sussex, Holt, Rinehart & Winston, 1980

And finally . . .

Like many management techniques, scheduling methods such as Gantt charts are not problem solving devices. They represent effective solutions to scheduling problems which facilitate planning and control. The representation of various situations in picture form will help answer managers' questions, and will help them choose the correct course of action and then evaluate that course of action. Thus, the chart shift-workers carry in their pockets showing their team's shift patterns represent a decision taken previously to utilize y numbers of shifts of z numbers of people within that unit. Scheduling techniques serve the purpose of planning, controlling and evaluating activities which the organization has decided already to undertake.

E   Monitoring

The fifth of our groupings is how to answer the question "Is it going according to plan?" When you have taken all the right decisions and influenced all the appropriate people to use the right administrative procedures, there remains the issue of whether or not the decisions are being implemented in the way intended, whether or not they are having the effect intended and, generally, how things are going. This is the management activity of monitoring.

The chapters here deal with a mixture of accounting and statistical methods of monitoring performance and presenting the performance data in the most cogent way possible.

It is important that monitoring is used as a check on policy. The temptation in policy-making is to adopt strategies that make sense in the light of prevailing circumstances, changing the strategy when the circumstances change. A change in the law, for instance, is the spur to a new policy initiative. The value of monitoring is that it can indicate the effectiveness of policies introduced already and suggest modifications without regarding policy innovation as solely responding to crises or external events in a reactive, defensive way. In some organizations there is a monthly supply of "control data", some of which is highly confidential and known only to the élite, while some of it is more general and all too often delivered in three or four pounds' weight of computer print-out. Our aim in this part of the book is to provide valid monitoring methods for individual managers running their own departments, as well as providing them with the ability to deal with those administering the centralized, organization-wide controls. Do not let accountants patronize you as they talk about budget-ary control; patronize them, instead, with a few well chosen and perceptive questions about cash flow!

42 Comparing performance with plan

In order for control of activities and operations to be exercised, constant comparison has to be made between expected and actual outcomes of plans. Knowledge of results is essential for understanding and progress. Without it, the manager could not improve the performance of the organization. Feedback signals the need for attention and corrective action on occasions when actual results deviate from those planned. However, feedback alone is insufficient without the existence of targets against which performance is to be judged and the presence of people who are in a position to take remedial action.

Other chapters deal extensively with the monitoring and control of individual performance (*see* section C) and of administrative procedures (*see* section D), whilst later chapters in this section describe specific techniques for the evaluation against plan of some other organizational activities. It is intended here to describe the workings of feedback and control systems in more general detail and in the context of managerial control.

Much has been made in this book about the need to set goals and objectives. If managers are to be able to compare performance with plans, targets must be set not only in connection with the performance levels expected but also for the nature and frequency of measures to be taken and for the amount of acceptable deviation from plan for each of these measures. In the evaluation of the customer services section, the manager will set targets for quality and reliability, timing and cost as measured by, for example, the proportion of goods supplied to customers which are within given and/or acceptable standards of design and performance, delay and price ranges.

Once performance levels are known to be outside the set acceptable standards, the manager must take decisions on the appropriate remedial action. Factors to be taken into account will include the reasons for the deviation; whether this is due to chance or some other uncontrollable variable such as the weather or a whim of fashion, or whether it is due to inferior/superior performance in any area, thus indicating the need for a change in the input balance. Positive deviations should not be excluded from detailed examination, of course. Departures from targeted performance levels may indicate a need for fuller explanation of the job, reassignment of duties, better training, additional staffing, more effective leadership or a redrawing of plans or modification of goals.

Some feedback and control mechanisms are automatic and self-regulating. The thermostat on the boiler or the automatic stock re-ordering system are examples of measures being taken, relayed and acted upon immediately and without human intervention. Not all performance is as easily-measurable as this, however. For example, feelings that the organization is failing to attract and keep the right calibre of workforce or that the marketing department is not keeping up with fashion are at first sight difficult to measure. The existence of quantified objectives and a well thought out control system in all the organization's activities, whether in marketing, production, research, finance or personnel, will assist managers in the process of comparing performance to plan even in those areas where measurement is less easy to quantify.

Closed feedback and control system (simplified)

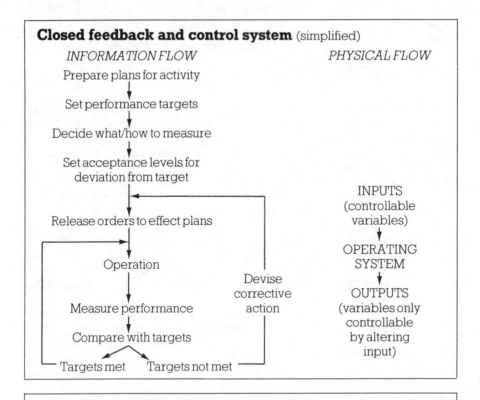

INFORMATION FLOW

Prepare plans for activity

Set performance targets

Decide what/how to measure

Set acceptance levels for
deviation from target

Release orders to effect plans

Operation

Measure performance

Compare with targets

Targets met   Targets not met

Devise
corrective
action

PHYSICAL FLOW

INPUTS
(controllable
variables)

OPERATING
SYSTEM

OUTPUTS
(variables only
controllable
by altering
input)

Some conventional control systems

Control area	Objectives of control (these should be as precisely defined as possible)	Feedback devices
Sales	To achieve forecast sales levels	Sales reports
Production	To maximize the efficiency of the work system	Reports of amounts of work in progress, proportion of orders completed on time and resource utilization
Stocks	To establish and maintain optimum stock levels at minimum cost	Reports on stock turn-round time, number of stock-out occasions.
Budgets	To keep expenditure and profits within required limits	Reports on expenditure and receipts
Personnel	To maximize personal and organizational performance	Appraisal reports and management by objectives, team briefing

Criteria for the setting of controls

Operational and procedural controls only come into effect when events need to be constrained in order to follow plans. They are checks and balances to make sure the system is functioning smoothly and to the correct standards.

According to Drucker (*op. cit.*) they should be:

ECONOMIC   Controls exist for an economic, not a moral purpose. They apply to the work of the organization; not to the workers. Their use should be minimized and confined to those occasions when it is necessary to examine the workings of the system.

APPROPRIATE   Energy should be put where it matters. Use the 80/20 rule: this states that, for example, 80 per cent of product costs are incurred by only 20 per cent of all items. Only in the important areas should highly rigorous control procedures be implemented.

REALISTIC   Controls should always relate to objectives; they should never measure trivial facts; and should never convey false accuracy or carry unnecessary precision. For example, a measure of up or down may be more significant than a specific figure correct to four decimal places.

SIMPLE   Complicated measures only confuse and misdirect energy away from what is being controlled to the control mechanism itself.

TIMELY   Frequent measurement should be taken, or rapid feedback used, only when absolutely necessary. For example, the evaluation of stock procedures requires a more instant feedback than do research activities.

OPERATIONAL   The results of control measures should be passed, in an appropriate and understandable format, to all those with authority and responsibility to act. This does not necessarily mean top management, but rather shop floor and office workers, supervisors and first line management.

Exercises

1 Imagine that you have decided to rationalize the procedure for the requisition of office equipment in your department. Devise an implementation plan to include your objectives, the performance targets you are seeking and the acceptable deviations, and the monitoring methods you intend to use during the early and later months of the operation of the new system.

2 Note down all the formal and informal control systems used in your department. Do you feel they should be used more/less rigorously? Why?

3 How much feedback do you give to and receive from your superiors? How much do you give to and receive from your subordinates? Consider ways in which you might improve the flow of information both upwards and downwards.

Further reading

BURBIDGE J L. *The Principles of Production Control*. 2nd ed. London, Macdonald & Evans, 1968

DRUCKER P F. *Management: Tasks, Responsibilities, Practices*. London, Wm Heinemann, 1974

GOLDSMITH W & CLUTTERBUCK D. *The Winning Streak*. London, Weidenfeld & Nicolson, 1984

TOWNSEND R. *Further Up the Organisation*. London, Michael Joseph, 1984

And finally . . .

Goldsmith and Clutterbuck found that a common factor of control in successful companies was constant feedback of results. Feedback to employees at all levels regarding output and performance gives them tools for self measurement and self direction. It provides them with the facts, not just judgements expressed in terms of praise or rebuke. Employees should be treated as concerned adults: bad or contentious news should be passed on as well as success stories, and questions should be answered directly and honestly. Team briefing (*see* chapter 17) should include a progress report related to both local and organizational objectives. The open passage of feedback both up and down the line is likely to generate a great deal of useful information.

43 Trends and predictions

Predictions may often lay the foundation for a company's entire business plan. Poor forecasting or the inappropriate application of forecasts will lead to wasted investment in stock, plant, equipment, materials and labour, and to lost revenue either due to forced cost cutting activities or out of stock situations.

Most forecasting activities rely on a formal analysis of past data to predict the future. Underlying movements of data over the years are identified and projected into the future, using methods of varying degrees of sophistication and complexity. The more unstable supply and demand movements are, the more important and more difficult accurate forecasting becomes, and the more elaborate the procedures need to be. Even though many of the techniques will be left to the company analysts or computer experts, it is important that managers have an understanding of them, so that they are aware both of the limitations of current methods and of the existence of other, perhaps better, methods. There will be many occasions also on which managers will choose to reject rigid rules and procedures in favour of a more entrepreneurial approach.

The main objective of forecasting techniques is to bring together all information and judgements relating to the problem in a logical, unbiased and systematic way. Where data are scarce, qualitative analysis will need to be used. In most cases, however, a combination of both qualitative and quantitative techniques is desirable. It is often of positive benefit to view the same problem from several different approaches. For example, when analyzing sales trends, managers can consult sales representatives, hold a conference of experts, and carry out a series of statistical analyses. The results of these various exercises can then be compared and, if appropriate, combined.

The formal use of trend analysis and prediction techniques within an organization plays an important part in encouraging dialogue between managers. Freeman claims that this serves the purpose of "mobilizing, energizing and organizing" future activity by becoming the organization's "tribal war-dances".

Prediction of what might happen is, of course, only the first step in the forecasting process. Decisions have to be made as to how to secure the resources needed to accommodate the predicted outcomes, and to ensure that the objectives set in the light of these estimates are met in the years ahead. It is important, therefore, that predictions are as realistic as possible.

Strategic planning requires managers to make decisions about the commitment of resources to the future in as systematic, as organized, and as purposeful a manner as possible. It requires the application of thought, imagination and judgement, both to the analysis of information and to the acceptance and taking of risks. Risk cannot, and indeed often should not, be eliminated. However, it can be identified, understood and applied rationally, and in this way used to improve the entrepreneurial decision-making capacity of management. Prediction techniques, whilst not capable of determining the future, help managers to identify those outcomes which are surrounded by greater or lesser amounts of uncertainty. Too great a dependence on statistical evidence at the expense of judgement can furnish a course of action with a credibility and legitimacy which can be harmful to the organization.

Trend analysis and prediction techniques

1 *QUANTITATIVE*   Data gathered for past periods are analyzed to find out what may have affected the results.

  i *Time series analysis*

A time series is any set of figures relating to the changing value of a variable over time.
A time series will usually have some or all of the following features:

Seasonal variations	Regular, annually repeated movements due to the effect of the seasons on the variable
Cyclical variations	Regular, long term patterns such as economic boom/depressions or product life cycles
Period variations	Movements in data due to the days of the week in the period or the number of weekends
A trend	An overall tendency for values to rise, fall or remain static
Random variations	Irregular fluctuations in values which fit no other pattern

These variations are isolated, and their effect separated from the data using various statistical techniques, such as moving averages, exponential smoothing, cumulative sum methods, standard deviations, etc. The data are thus presented in a re-adjusted fashion so that the true movement of the figures is revealed.

 ii *Associative indicators*

There are often relationships which exist between sets of data which can provide some indication of the extent to which knowledge of the value of one variable is useful for the prediction of the value of another. However, it should be remembered that although statistical analysis may show a positive relationship between two sets of data, this is not proof that one has caused the other.

These relationships are identified by statistical methods such as correlation and regression analysis.

Trend analysis and prediction techniques continued

2 *QUALITATIVE*   Opinions and judgements regarding predictions and trends are sought from well informed experts, from within and outside the company.

  i *The Delphi technique* (consulting the 'oracle')

   Selected individuals are asked about their estimates and assumptions by means of a questionnaire, often very precise and detailed. Their written responses are coordinated into a 'consensus' view. This is then returned to the individuals with a request to maintain, modify and justify their original judgements. The process is continued, with no contact between the experts, until the considered, personal opinion of each one coincides to form one viewpoint.

  ii *Panel consensus*

   Selected experts meet to discuss the issue and to arrive at a group view. The interplay of ideas is encouraged and the method relies on the assumption that cooperation between several people will give rise to a more accurate analysis than that offered by the isolated individual. (See also the advantages of group over individual problem-solving in chapter 8.)

Obstacles to the use of trend analysis techniques

In his investigations of technological forecasting practice, Freeman (*op. cit.*) found that organizations that could have benefitted from formal prediction techniques often did not use them. He found that the obstacles to their use were due frequently to lack of management commitment, and included the following:

1 failure to integrate forecasting activities as a whole into the organization's regular planning programme;

2 failure to be objective in planning – advocacy and political debate used instead;

3 failure to understand and welcome analysis techniques;

4 failure by top management to support forecasting efforts;

5 failure of management to look into the long term.

Exercises

1 Think of a forecasting problem in your organization. Note down which elements of the problem would be suited to a) quantitative and b) qualitative analysis.

2 Find out how much trend analysis and prediction activity takes place in your own department, and in other departments. Is it formally organized? If so, how is it organized? If not, can you pinpoint the reasons?

3 To what extent are computer programs used in your organization for trend analysis activities? Do you know what software is available in the market to aid managers in these tasks? Find out, if you do not know.

Further reading

FREEMAN C. *The Economics of Industrial Innovation*. 2nd ed. London, Frances Pinter (Publishers) Ltd, 1982

HARPER W M. *Statistics*. 4th ed. Plymouth, Devon, Macdonald & Evans, 1982 (M & E Handbooks)

HARRIS J & POWELL J. *Quantitative Decision Making*. Harlow, Essex, Longman, 1982. (Understanding Business)

KOTLER P. *Marketing Management: Analysis, Planning & Control*. 4th ed. Englewood Cliffs, NJ, Prentice Hall, 1980

WILD R. *Production and Operations Management: Principles and Techniques*. Eastbourne, Sussex, Holt, Rinehart & Winston Ltd, 1979

And finally . . .

An important question to be asked before sophisticated trend analysis and prediction exercises are undertaken is whether the time and effort expended in the process is worth the benefits gained. Where decisions are of a short term nature and can be changed or reversed with little or no expense, a simple cost/benefit review might indicate that an intelligent guess would serve the purpose quite adequately. On the other hand, decisions which are long term or expensive to change justify the devotion of resources.

44 Departmental budgetary control

The management functions of planning, controlling and evaluating performance have many financial aids. Budgets are detailed plans of action for an organization for the forthcoming period expressed in financial terms, and are among the most commonly used management tools.

As a tool of managerial control, budgeting serves three important purposes. First, it imposes a duty upon members of the department to quantify objectively their targets and performance levels; secondly, it provides criteria for the judgement of performance; thirdly, it promotes communication and coordination.

Without planned targets, the department's operations lack direction, unforeseen problems occur, departmental results lack meaning, and the importance of keeping an eye on the future gives way to the pressures of the moment. Budgets provide the manager with a means of controlling the direction of the activities of the department, and in turn the direction of the whole organization. Managers need to convince their staff that budgets serve a positive role in the improvement of the department and of the company. When incorporated into personal targets (for example, using management by objectives techniques), they can also play a positive role in the development and progress of individual members of the department. Ideally, the budget should indicate the person accountable for each item of expenditure.

The level of the departmental budget may be determined in various ways. 'Rule of thumb' measures, such as a percentage increase on the previous year's budget, are an irrational approach and indicate that the budget is not being used as a serious planning tool. Budget levels should instead be set using an objective, task orientated approach, which considers organizational goals and the means of achieving these goals.

Budgeting provides the manager with a means of checking progress to determine whether plans are being fulfilled. If monitored expenditures exceed or fall short of budgeted levels, the manager is alerted to possible deviations from planned performance levels. Whilst the budget provides an early warning system for danger and lack of performance, it also highlights opportunities when performance is better than expected. Managers should spend as much time on the healthy areas as on the problem areas. However, budgets should be flexibly and prudently administered by the manager, and not regarded as a strait jacket. Their purpose is to try to guide the department towards its planned objectives: they should be respected but not revered.

Budgeting also serves as an important communication and integration device. The departmental budget highlights operational relationships within the department and with other departments. It prevents empire building tendencies by broadening individual thinking processes. It helps eliminate confused responsibilities and working relationships both outside and within the department and, finally, it provides a framework for that most vital of control methods, feedback. The budgeting process is thus a further example of an organization's "tribal dances" (*see* chapter 43).

If managers prepare and use budgets with care, commitment and confidence within a positive organizational environment, that organization is likely to perform better than one which does not budget.

The budgeting planning cycle

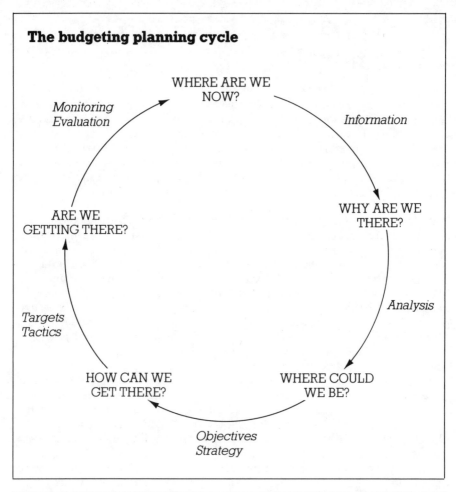

WHERE ARE WE
NOW?

*Monitoring
Evaluation*

Information

ARE WE
GETTING THERE?

WHY ARE WE
THERE?

Analysis

*Targets
Tactics*

HOW CAN WE
GET THERE?

WHERE COULD
WE BE?

*Objectives
Strategy*

Budget classifications

CAPITAL EXPENDITURE — Plant and equipment, tax deductable only to the amount they are depreciated each year

EXPENSES — Salaries, travel expenses, advertising, entertainment, production materials and other overheads; wholly deductable for tax purposes

CASH — Payments and receipts (*see* chapter 49)

Preparation of the budget

1 Forecasts covering departmental activities in physical terms are prepared by individual managers, using the planning cycle outlined previously.

2 Top management checks the compatibility of all departmental forecasts to ensure, for example, that forecasts for production and stock levels tie up with those for sales, labour and machine capacities. Compatibility with overall organizational objectives is also checked.

3 Individual forecasts are expressed in financial terms using organizational and economic guidelines, and with the assistance of the company's financial accountants. Decisions may be taken at this stage to remove factors such as machine capacities which may limit the scale of activities, with due regard to the cost and benefit of doing so. Decisions also may be made not to proceed with certain activities.

4 Individual forecasts are scrutinized by top management or by the budget committee. The master forecast is compared with organizational objectives, and a decision made as to whether it is acceptable.

5 The master forecast receives formal approval, and each departmental forecast then becomes a budget, representing the formal policy of the department, and becoming an instruction to members of the department.

Adapted from Harvey and Nettleton, *Management Accounting, op. cit.*

Other types of budgets

Zero based budgeting
This method of departmental budgeting requires managers to justify every item of the expenditure proposed, as though it is a brand new project which is under consideration. Its aim is to pinpoint priorities, eliminate unnecessary expenditure and unproductive activities.

Life cycle budgeting
With many activities, it is unrealistic to expect the financial commitment to be confined to a single year, eg capital projects, research and development, management training, sales promotion and advertising. These activites should be budgeted on a life basis, showing the levels of expenditure needed over the duration of the activity. The manager should always budget for maximum success; the successful programme will require more, not less, resources in future years.

Flexible budgets
These are budgets which allow for changing levels of performance of sales and production which may give rise to different levels of costs. A set of budgets is constructed at several levels of volume, showing what costs they incur at these different levels.

Exercises

1 Who prepares your departmental budget? How is the whole budgeting process carried out? Do you have a procedural budget manual, or budget committees? If not, how do you ensure a uniformity of approach and presentation?

2 Make sure that budget statements are produced and made public every month, or at least every quarter, showing separately the items with significant deviations from forecast. What is your criterion for deciding whether the deviation requires action?

3 Is the budget incorporated into the tasks and targets for individual members of staff on an annual basis?

4 If it is not already done, request top management to give regular briefings to all staff on the organization's master budget and the achievement (or otherwise) of that budget.

Further reading

DRUCKER P F. *Management*. London, Pan, 1979

HARVEY D A & NETTLETON M. *Management Accounting*. London, Mitchell Beazley, 1983 (Core Business Studies)

HORNGREN C T. *Cost Accounting: A Managerial Emphasis*. 5th ed. Englewood Cliffs, NJ, Prentice Hall Inc, 1982

WOOD F & TOWNSLEY J. *Managerial Accounting and Finance*. Stockport, Cheshire, Polytech Publishers Ltd, 1983

And finally . . .

The importance of obtaining the commitment of all members of the organization to the budgeted objectives is vital. Horngren suggests that "the success of a budgetary system depends on its acceptance by the company members who are affected by the budgets". Individual members on whom a budget is imposed, rather than those who have an active part in its drafting, are likely to pay it little attention or will abuse its control functions. Managers should ensure that their budgets are prepared at working level in order to make certain that the members of the department believe the budget to be workable. Top management should demonstrate also their belief in the budgeting process of the company, since the overall master forecast will show the actions management is taking to influence the future direction of the company.

45 Sampling methods

Sampling is taking examples of events, objects or people to represent the whole. Probably the best known samples are opinion polls where one thousand people are asked their political opinions and the newspapers then claim Labour have X percent, Conservatives Y percent and the Alliance Z percent of the vote. It is important that the sample is a reasonable representation of the whole population so that the results can be generalized. Sampling is necessary when it is impracticable to measure, test, talk with or describe every event, object or person. This may be because of lack of time, shortage of money or because the process is continuous whereas the measurement is discrete.

Sampling is a useful method for managers in a variety of tasks. Managers in marketing and sales departments will use it to test new products and advertising campaigns on a sample of the population before committing a large budget. Service industries, including public sector organizations, will sample their clients to ensure the public are satisfied and, if not, where the problems exist: personnel departments may sample the employees for their opinions on whether to upgrade the staff restaurant or the sports facilities; work study departments will sample the working practices to identify difficulties; quality control will sample the production, whether batch or continuous, to identify whether the product is up to standard; technical services will take samples of the problem product to take away for analysis, and so forth.

Statisticians call the whole group the population, or universe, and the proportion of this is called the sample. The validity of this sample can be biased in either of two ways. Firstly, by including examples that are not part of the population, for example, the marketing department may test a new cat food advertisement on someone who does not own a cat; or technical services might take a sample for analysis from the batch that is not giving problems. Secondly, the sample can be biased by not being representative of the population. For instance using the telephone directory to sample the population about health services does not include the views of those without telephones, largely the less well off; or if quality control sample a manufacturing process only after lunch, it will not indicate whether the goods are equally well made throughout the day.

There are no upper or lower limits to a sample size. Where statistical techniques are used they may set a minimum number. Otherwise, it is the amount of work and expense that can be justified, since both increase with sample size and yet each extra member of the sample has less impact than the previous one. So a judgement has to be made as to the most appropriate sample size. It helps to ask the all-important question, "What are the consequences if this sample is an incorrect representation of the whole?". The more critical accuracy is, the greater the expense in time and money is justified and so the larger the sample can be.

Sampling methods

RANDOM SAMPLE selected by pure chance from the population

1 Number each event, person or period of time

2 Toss a coin, take every tenth, pull name from hat or look at random figure tables or computer generated figures

3 Measure, ask, test those whose number comes up

Test Does every name or thing in the whole group have an equal chance to be in the sample.
Example Using random figure tables to determine which objects are taken from the production line for testing; giving every tenth guest a questionnaire to complete on hotel facilities and service

QUOTA OR STRATIFIED SAMPLE selected to fit a particular description

1 List the characteristics of the whole population, particularly as they would affect the issue to be sampled

2 Decide how many you can afford to sample

3 Make sure that each of the characteristics is represented in similar proportions to the population

4 Measure, test, ask those who fit the criteria

Test Is your description of the whole population accurate; particularly with reference to the current issue?
Example Taking the first, twentieth and last example from the production line after each process for quality control; market researchers making sure they have 5 twenty-year olds, 5 thirty-year olds, and so on

BELLWETHER SAMPLE a known sub-set that represents the population closely

1 Look at previous samples and the results they gave

2 Select the most accurate sample

3 Ensure the present purpose is similar and that nothing much has changed since last time

4 Measure, ask, test the same sample

Test Has the population changed since the previous sampling?
Example Take sample from production at 3pm as that is when problems usually arise. The viewing panel, who are the sample on which viewing figures are based for television, is a carefully selected cross section of the public used to ascertain popularity ratings.

Sampling error

Various statistical techniques have been developed to test the likelihood of the sample being significantly different from the population. These tests can be used only where the measurement, descriptions, tests and opinions are numerically recorded.

If sufficient examples of an event, behaviour or process are measured and the results plotted on a graph the shape of the curve tends towards the normal distribution curve. Various mathematical laws are known about this curve. An important one is that 66⅔% of the population is within 1 SD of the mean, 95% within 2 SD and 99¾% within 3 SD. (SD =Standard Deviation – a measure of how spread out the curve is from the mean or average). The formula for calculating a SD is $\sqrt{\dfrac{(\varepsilon x - \bar{x})^2}{n}}$

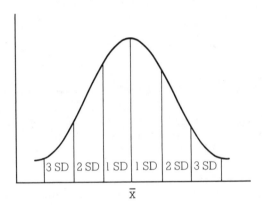

$$\bar{x}$$

By comparing the results from the sample with the known laws of normal curves a test is made of whether there is a significant difference between the sample and the population. That is, can the results be relied on as representing the whole group?.

There are a wide range of statistical tests available, each with particular characteristics suitable for certain circumstances. 't' tests are widely used for a variety of sample sizes, to test whether there is a statistically significant difference between the sample and the population. The particular formulae will vary with sample size and type of measure used. χ^2 is used for comparing an observed set of values with what might be expected and whether there is a statistically significant difference between them. The formulae for χ^2 varies depending how many things are compared. The formulae for 't' tests and χ^2 will be found in any statistical book or computer statistics programme.

Exercises

1 If you wanted to know how people voted in the last election, which of the following methods would be most appropriate and why: ask all householders at their doors; telephone everyone listed in the telephone book; telephone every other one; knock on every other householder's door; describe population in terms of age, sex, income, type of house and find sample in proportion; randomly interview those listed on the electoral roll.

2 A chemical plant works on a continual process. When is it most cost effective to take quality assurance samples. What factors need to be considered?

Further reading

HARPER W M. 4th ed. *Statistics*. London, Macdonald and Evans, 1982
HUFF D. *How to Lie with Statistics*. Harmondsworth, Middx., Penguin, 1954
ROBSON E. *Experiment, Design and statistics in psychology*, Harmondsworth, Middx., Penguin, 1973

And finally . . .

Samples that are not carefully selected can lead to nonsense. For example, overheard remarks can be amusing, precisly because they are not a true sample of the conversation. Standing on their own, these statements acquire unintended meanings. Nigel Rees has collected some of these, where the context is impossible to fathom (Rees, N. *Eavesdropping*, Hemel Hempstead, Herts., Unwin, 1981)

When I do it I tend to catch my fingers on the floorboards (p. 14 *op. cit.*)

There are only two in the whole of Guildford and one is covered with ants (p. 21 *op. cit.*)

46 Graphs and diagrams

Most of us are able to see spatial relationships more clearly than numerical relationships. If you find yourself with a lot of figures to compare, you might well start by putting it into some sort of tabular order. Turning the data into pictures may be a further improvement still, particularly if you are looking at comparative trends or proportions. Visual presentation may provide you with a summary as a basis for discussion or may serve simply to clarify a situation in your own mind.

Your audience may feel, with some justification, that you can prove anything you wish with statistics. You should avoid overwhelming people with a vast amount of complex pictures, therefore. Use visual presentation of statistics, not primarily as illumination, but as support for your case in the form of intelligent backup to written or oral argument or demonstration.

Visual presentation methods can be divided into two main groups: graphs and diagrams. The former is the representation of data by means of a continuous line set within two axes, whilst the latter includes many different forms of visual representation, including bar charts, pie charts and pictorial representation. Whichever method you choose may well depend on personal preference. There are obviously some media which are more suited to certain forms. For example, pie charts are useful for the simple presentation of a large number of component percentages but are little use for showing the increase in volume in aggregated data; bar charts are useful for depicting values in up to four individual components, since the height and length of each bar is proportionate to the magnitudes represented; pictograms present an elementary, yet attractive, form of visual representation useful for presenting changes in total data to a relatively uninformed and undemanding audience; graphs, on the other hand, are frequently used for displaying trends over long periods of time since each point of time occupies relatively little space.

There are many refinements to these basic kinds of statistical presentation which can be used to illustrate specific phenomena, such as frequency distributions, inequalities and relativities. Once you get more used to the examination and presentation of data in an illustrative form, these refinements are worth using. Most basic statistics textbooks describe them in some detail. It is better, however, to use the basic methods competently and accurately than to misuse the more complex methods.

Whether you are a journalist or an advertising copywriter, a speaker at a conference or a report writer, and whether the information you are seeking to present concerns earnings, market growth, geographical distribution, demand levels, percentage population or profit margins, you will probably find your task made easier by the selective use of a graph or diagram. As well as providing instant visual impact to the presentation of comparisons, trends, growth patterns, etc, a diagram in a company report will provide respite for the reader's eye whilst a graphical representation on an overhead projector will offer the viewer a welcome break from concentrated listening.

Simple principles of graph construction

1 A good presentation will be well-defined and undistorted and, therefore, will seek to give an accurate picture of the information. Figure 2 makes a modest rise of 10 per cent in costs look like a disaster. Those who wish to win arguments, to amaze or alarm the viewer or to sell an idea may resort to this tactic. However, if you genuinely wish to convey information, stick to the method used in Figure 1: start your vertical scale with zero and show all the scale points.

If you really do not have enough space, make it clear that there is a definite break in the scale (as shown in Figure 3).

2 Make it clear what the graph is representing (units, time scales, etc). Give it a clear title and label both axes or, while people try to work out exactly what is being put across, you will have defeated the purpose of choosing a visual representation.

3 Independent variables (those unaffected by changes in the other variable, eg month, year, age) should be placed on the horizontal axis.

4 Make all the lines distinct. Use colours or differently drawn lines (eg dotted) where there are several lines. The thickness of the line is unlikely to matter: if accurate values are needed, the original data can still be referred to.

5 Limit the number of lines on one display to avoid confusion or loss of visual clarity.

6 Give the source of data so that details of figures can be obtained, or write the actual figure on the graph itself.

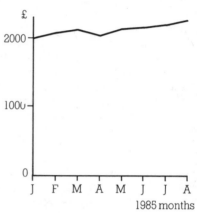

Figure 1
Paper consumption costs
Reprographics Dept
(monthly returns)

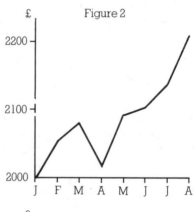

Figure 2

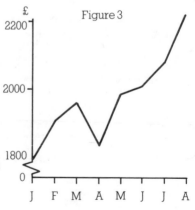

Figure 3

Simple principles of bar chart construction

1 Keep the widths of bars constant, otherwise the volume of the bar will be difficult to compare and the meaning lost.

2 See also the principles for graph construction (but note that the 'break to zero' should never be used in bar charts since it is the correct impression of volume that is important).

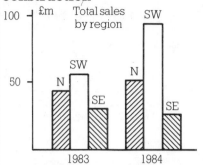

Simple principles of pie chart construction

1 Each segment of the circle is proportional to the size of the figure represented.

2 To construct a pie chart, calculate the angles at the centre of the 'pie' by multiplying each percentage component by 360 degrees (eg if one component is 20 per cent of the total figure, the angle at the centre is $\frac{20}{100} \times 360 = 72$ degrees).
Divisions can thus be drawn easily with the use of a calculator and a protractor.

3 Limit the number of components shown to seven or eight.

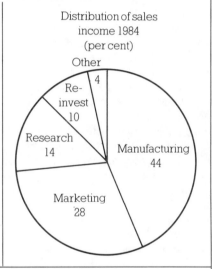

Simple principles of pictogram construction

1 Comparative values are represented by variation in the size or number of objects.

2 Use of a varying number of pictures of the same size is preferable to using one drawing of different sizes. With the latter, there may be confusion over whether it is height or width that is being read, eg a doubling in height usually involves a doubling in width also, which may appear as a quadrupling of volume (or an increase by a factor of eight with a three-dimensional picture).

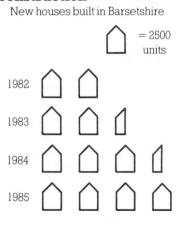

Exercises

1 In the first six months of 1984, averages for exports to main markets were as follows (in £ million): EEC 138, Australia 122, USA 46, Africa 8, Others 61. Construct a pie chart to represent these figures.

2 Plot both sets of figures, relating to sunshine and profits on suntan lotion, on the same graph using a double scale, one on the left vertical axis and one on the right. Choose scales which result in the two curves occupying similar parts of the graph, eg sunshine 0-8 hrs, profits £0-1000.

Period	1	2	3	4	5	6	7	8	9	10
Sunshine (hours per day)	6.1	7.3	6.5	5.8	4.9	4.1	5.5	8.0	7.3	6.8
Profits (£)	621	740	894	773	702	591	488	661	992	863

3 Depict the data below in the form of a component bar chart:

subjects studies at XYZ Commercial College, 1985
(numbers of students)

Professional 1230, comprising Accounting 910, Banking 212,
    Management 108
Languages 572, comprising French 302, German 245, Italian 25
Academic 441, comprising O levels 332, A levels 93, degrees 16.

Further reading

HARPER W M. *Statistics*. 4th ed. Plymouth, Devon, Macdonald & Evans, 1982 (M & E Handbooks)
HUFF D. *How to Lie with Statistics*. Harmondsworth, Middx., Penguin, 1973
YEOMANS K A. *Introducing Statistics*. Harmondsworth, Middx., Penguin, 1968 (Studies in Applied Statistics)

And finally ...

Of course, new technology has the ability instantly to convert numerical data into pictures at the flick of a switch. Search through any micro-computer software catalogue and you will find a program which allows you to select a picture type and which will display the chosen graphic on screen using data supplied. The same data can, for example, be transformed into pie charts, vertical or horizontal bar charts or graphs, by the use of just one business graphics software package.

47 Personnel indicators

In this section of the book we have a series of methods for monitoring organizational performance. They are mainly statistical and other measures, but we describe here some general indicators that give early warning of matters which may be affecting employee effectiveness. The two broad categories of indicator are the *survey* and the *trend*. The survey is an attempt to understand some aspect of what is happening in the here and now, while the trend is a regular monitoring of how indicators are changing week by week or month by month through the accumulation and analysis of a large number of frequent incidents.

Some surveys are of demographic data, like the distribution of employees' ages, their sex, racial and ethnic origin, and length of service. In very large undertakings this information may be substantial enough to warrant trend analyses, but usually the data is considered periodically by managers to check the satisfactoriness of the manpower profile. Is there an adequate distribution of ages across the range of jobs, or is remedial action needed to prevent a shortage at some future stage? Is there any indication that women or members of minority groups are being blocked at promotion points?

The attitude survey is a deliberate attempt to find out employee attitudes to features of the business and its management. These have never been widely used and they present problems, such as the discovery of a widespread dissatisfaction on some matter which the management feels unable to meet. Would it have been wiser not to open that particular 'can of worms'? Attitude surveys can be useful, but they raise expectations. Also some employees suspect such questioning and may not be prepared to provide the answers.

The main trends to be monitored are absence and turnover. Out of a normal 250 working days in a year, employees are likely to be absent for between 10 per cent and 30 per cent of that time, for authorized or unauthorized absence. Both have to be monitored. One organization has given us the following average figures for its employees over 12 months:

annual holiday	20 days
training and education	5 days
miscellaneous authorized (funerals, jury duty etc)	2 days
sickness and other absence	9 days

These need to be monitored individually to ensure that the sickness absence is genuine and the annual holiday arrangements do not leave a department unable to operate, but they also need to be monitored for the trends, which then can be compared between departments and for the same period in the previous year. With the relatively tight labour market of the present time, turnover or wastage is not as big a problem as it used to be, and some employers feel that their turnover level is too low rather than too high. It still remains a useful general indicator. Absence and turnover levels can be compared also with published figures, in the Department of Employment *Gazette* and the *General Household Survey*, which provide information on the general characteristics of different regions and industries.

Other trend indicators are only likely to be useful in very large organizations where there is a great deal of data to analyze: days lost through industrial action, number of grievances registered, number of accidents, and amount of lost time.

Measuring absence 1   lost time

This shows the percentage of working time that has been lost through employee absence over a given period of time.

$$\frac{\text{Number of days lost through absence}}{\text{Average number of employees} \times \text{number of days}} \times 100$$

Example: In a workforce of 80, two people are absent for one whole day each and 10 are absent for half a day each, over a period of five days.

$$\frac{7}{80 \times 5} \times 100 = 1.75\%$$

Measuring absence 2   frequency

This shows the extent of the absence across the workforce by showing the number of times people are absent. This can be a useful refinement as frequent short absences can be a bigger problem than rarer long spells.

$$\frac{\text{Number of absences}}{\text{Average number of employees}} \times 100$$

Example: Using the same figures as in the first example,

$$\frac{12}{80} \times 100 = 15\%$$

Measuring turnover 1   separation

The number of people leaving the organization or department is shown as a percentage of the total establishment.

$$\frac{\text{Number of leavers}}{\text{Number of employees}} \times 100$$

Example: Over a period, 85 people leave from a workforce of 300.

$$\frac{85}{300} \times 100 = 28.3\%$$

Measuring turnover 2   stability

As many of those who leave organizations do so in the early weeks of employment, it can be useful to measure the underlying stability by using the formula

$$\frac{\text{Number of employees with more than 12 months service}}{\text{Average number of employees}} \times 100$$

Attitude survey

Questions in an attitude survey need to be related to current practice in the organization and on matters about which the management needs information. Here are some general questions that might be a starting point for developing a more precise survey. Respondents are asked to tick one of the columns against each statement.

	strongly agree	agree	no opinion	disagree	strongly disagree
Management treatment of employees is fair					
Managers have a firm grip on operations					
If you have a problem you can rely on the departmental manager to get something done					
Employees' views are seldom considered by management when changes are being made					
The work I have to do is generally interesting and satisfying					
I find the atmosphere in my department a pleasant one to work in					
The equipment and materials we have to work with are efficient and well-maintained					
Rates of pay here are better than in most other companies nearby					
Pay differentials between departments are not fair					
I would work harder if there was an incentive scheme					
The company is generally doing well at the moment					
We are well-trained for the work we have to do					
There are good opportunities for promotion					

Any attitude survey should be piloted before use. A sample of the proposed respondents should be asked not only to answer the questions, but to comment on those they could not understand, did not trust or were not willing to answer. They may also suggest additional points to be included.

If people are asked to take part in a survey like this, they will expect to hear something of the outcome.

Exercise

There are 175 employees in a large office. Over an 8-week period individual employees are absent as follows:

	week 1	week 2	week 3	week 4	week 5	week 6	week 7	week 8
Absent 5 days	3	3	3	4	4	2	2	2
Absent 4 days	1	0	1	2	0	0	1	0
Absent 3 days	4	4	5	5	6	6	8	9
Absent 2 days	7	8	9	9	9	9	9	10
Absent 1 day	9	7	8	9	9	11	11	10
Absent ½ day	5	6	6	7	8	8	9	9
Absent 1 day twice	2	2	1	0	1	2	3	2
Absent ½ day twice	2	2	2	4	0	0	3	3
Absent ½ day three times	1	0	0	0	0	2	2	3
Absent 1 day once, ½ day once	2	4	0	4	3	4	4	5

Calculate the lost time for each week and the frequency for each week. How do these calculations improve your understanding of the position?

Further reading

ADVISORY, CONCILIATION and ARBITRATION SERVICE, *Labour Turnover*. Advisory Booklet No 4, 1984
ADVISORY, CONCILIATION and ARBITRATION SERVICE, *Absence*, Advisory Booklet No 5, 1985
CENTRAL STATISTICAL OFFICE. *Social Trends*. HMSO, published annually
DEPARTMENT OF EMPLOYMENT, *Gazette*. HMSO, published monthly

The first two publications cited above provide excellent brief summaries of approaches to both problems; the latter two provide regular comparative information about employment nationally, regionally and by industry, against which the trends for an individual business can be compared.

And finally . . .

The following statements are *generally* valid:

1 Younger employees have more short spells of absence than older employees; older employees are more likely to be off for long periods.
2 Except for maternity leave, there is little difference in the amount of sickness absence taken by men and women until the later years of employment when men are likely to lose more time.
3 Manual employees are more likely to be absent from work than white collar employees.
4 Among those with degree-level qualifications under the age of 35, turnover among men is higher than among women.
5 Absence is highest among those working shifts, heavy overtime and in large working groups.

48   Depreciation

Any decrease in capital resulting from operations is an expense which, when deducted from revenue, reduces the company's profits and, therefore, its ability to pay higher wages, finance new projects, build new plants and offices. Depreciation is such an expense; it is like a payment the company makes for the use of an asset over its life, somewhat like an annual rent charge. Fixed assets are likely to generate revenue over a number of years and their cost is spread accordingly. It is the process of allocating this cost that is depreciation.

Depreciation over the life of an asset can be described simply as its cost, less its value at the end of its useful life. Only one of these component elements, initial cost, can be determined objectively. Estimating the other two elements, the asset's useful life and its value, if any, at the end of its life, is often an inspired guess, based on the perceived reason for the decline in the value of the asset over the years and a capacity to predict the future.

Depreciation is applied particularly to machinery, vehicles and equipment. Freehold land and buildings may suffer depreciation but are more likely to maintain or increase their original cost level due to inflation and demand levels. However, appreciation of assets, unlike depreciation, seldom results in a change to the profits of the organization, largely due to the accountant's adherence to the concept of historical costing and concern with the convention of conservatism which understates, rather than overstates, the value of assets, with the compensatory spin-off of reducing liability for tax. Specific types of depreciation such as amortization and depletion, may be applied to other types of asset (*see* overleaf).

It can be seen that the whole process of assigning precise figures to depreciation is often quite arbitrary. There are specific methods, however, by which, once the three depreciation components have been established, depreciation is allocated on a year by year basis in a systematic and rational manner. One approach views the asset as equally available and capable of use over its whole life, with either constant or insignificant maintenance costs. This method allocates depreciation equally each year and is called the 'straight line method'. Another approach, used where the asset is most efficient in the early years, charges progressively smaller amounts of depreciation as the asset declines in efficiency and needs more maintenance. This method ensures that expenses charged against revenue are as evenly spread as possible, and is known as the 'reducing balance method'. The straight line method is the simplest and most widely used in this country, although many small firms use the reducing balance method since it can convey tax advantages.

Provision for depreciation does not, of course, affect the actual use of assets, but it is a business expense with resultant financial implications. According to the Accounting Standards Committee, the allocation of depreciation involves "the exercise of judgement by management in the light of technical, commercial and accounting considerations and accordingly requires annual review".

Causes of depreciation, depletion and amortization

Type of asset

1 *Physical deterioration*
Mechanical wear and tear, rusting | Machinery, plant, vehicles

Rot and decay, exposure to elements | Timber buildings

Erosion | Land

2 *Exhaustion of resources* (depletion)
Where raw materials such as minerals are being extracted from the asset | Mines, quarries, oil wells

3 *Passage of time* (amortization)
Associated with all other causes, but particularly where the legal life of the asset is fixed | Leases, patents, copyrights

4 *Economic factors*
Where an asset is put out of use despite its good condition
 i Obsolescence
 The asset, or the product or service which the asset helps to produce, becomes outdated owing to technological development, product life cycles, market forces, fashion | Computer cash registers, large cars, buggy whips, the corner shop, the internal combustion engine

 ii Inadequacy
 The asset is inappropriate to the task now assigned to it, due to changes in, or growth of, the organization | Warehousing, transport, production units

Typical life spans built into depreciation allowances are as follows: furniture and office equipment – 10 years; vehicles – four years; computers – three years; automated equipment – five years; manufacturing plant – 20 years; leasehold land/buildings – the remaining term of the lease.

Depreciation in final accounts

Since depreciation is an expense or loss to the business, it is entered as a debit in the profit and loss account. At the same time, the assets shown in the balance sheet are reduced in value.

Requirements for the disclosure of information regarding depreciation are set out in the Companies Act 1948, and in the Accounting Standards Committee's Statement of Standard Accounting Practice (SSAP 12). The following must be disclosed in the financial statement of the organization for each major class of depreciable asset:

1   the depreciation method used

2   the useful life, or depreciation rate used

3   the total depreciation allocated for the period

4   the gross amount of depreciable assets, and the accumulated depreciation.

It may well be the case that the asset lasts longer than its expected life, that its period of use is less than that expected, or that the amount received on disposal is more or less than the estimated amount. The actual use of the asset is not affected, but this means that the appropriate adjustments have to be included in the next financial statement to reflect the previous, incorrect estimates for depreciation provision.

Depreciation and CCA (current cost accounting)

Although depreciation is an allocation and not a valuation technique, it may seem anomalous that provision for depreciation, which effectively reduces the apparent value of an asset, is made when the real value of the asset is increasing due to rising price levels. In the conventional, historical cost method of accounting, depreciation is charged against current revenue but on the basis of the original historical cost of the asset. CCA (SSAP 16) seeks to reflect the impact of specific price changes on the value of assets shown in the final accounts. The revised value for depreciable fixed assets is arrived at by using relevant specified indices or open market value as appropriate to the class of asset. Since the revised value is likely to be higher than the historical cost, the CCA depreciation amount is also likely to be higher. The difference between the two is incorporated into CCA final accounts. The aim is to set aside enough resources to buy replacement fixed assets at current prices, which historical cost accounting does not achieve.

Exercises

1 Note down examples of fixed assets in your department/organization which fall under the four causes of depreciation listed on the page 194.

2 Work out the annual depreciation charge on your car using the following formula (the straight line method of calculating depreciation):

$$\frac{(\text{Historical cost} + \text{maintenance}) - \text{Estimated residual value}}{\text{Number of years of expected use}}$$

3 Obtain your organization's report and accounts and look for disclosure of the information listed on the previous page in the notes to the accounts and in the accounts themselves.

Further reading

HARVEY M & KEER F. *Financial Accounting Theory.* London, Prentice Hall, 1978
WOOD F. *Business Accounting 1.* 3rd ed. London, Longman, 1979

And finally . . .

Harvey & Keer (*op. cit.*) emphasize two factors regarding depreciation in historical cost accounting:

1 Depreciation does *not* provide a measure of the asset's current value: it is a process of allocating cost over the asset's life, not of valuation. Owners of small businesses seeking new finance from their bank managers will, in fact, find that their plant and stock are often valued at only half their depreciated amount.

2 Depreciation does *not* provide for the replacement of assets. The process of depreciation has indeed converted the asset back into cash over its useful life, but the replacement cost is likely to be higher and the cash theoretically released will probably have been invested in other assets. The provision of sufficient funds to replace expired assets is a task of cash flow management rather than of depreciation (see chapter 49).

49   Cash flow

It is essential for managers to know not only what the organization's profits are but also that its cash resources are sufficient to meet its commitments as they fall due. The lack of cash resources will in the short term limit the company's activities and freedom of action. With an inadequate level of liquid funds, the company will, for example, be unable to take advantage of unexpected opportunities. More seriously it will not be able to pay its suppliers, creditors, employees or shareholders. With a bad credit reputation, it will experience real survival problems. Surplus cash is an idle, and therefore wasted, resource.

In order that management is able to meet its commitments, cash budgets should be drawn up estimating the cash receipts and payments for each month. These will warn when cash shortages might be expected or will highlight cash surpluses, so that appropriate remedies may be taken. The planning and control of cash flow is a central element in the management of the business. There is little point in formally estimating costs for operational activities if the organization then runs out of cash funds for financing those activities. Cash budgeting emphasizes the relationship between operational plans and the financing of the business: managers have the ability of creating the need for cash as well as bringing in cash. The budget is an authorization also for the finance manager responsible for the management of funds, monitoring cash resources and alerting other managers to deviations (*see* chapter 44).

When considering the cash implications of the organization's activities, certain factors should be considered. For example, there will be a time lag between sales, purchases and production activities, and the payment or receipt of cash. Other expenses such as rates and insurance occur unevenly throughout the year, requiring careful planning. Furthermore, certain expenses such as depreciation do not result in a decrease of cash, even though they reduce the profit of the organization. Cash outgoings, such as the payment of dividends or tax, or the redemption of debts will, on the other hand, have no effect on profit.

Growing organizations financing new products, services, markets and acquisitions may need to increase their cash availability. Ways of doing this by reducing funds tied up in current assets, or releasing capital tied up in fixed assets, are listed overleaf. Managers should also examine their product portfolios and strategies. Products with a high market share have high cash generating abilities, but if they are in high growth markets will also have a high cash using requirement. 'Harvesting' strategies which aim at increasing cash flow in the short term by an emphasis on products which have a high market share in a static or declining market may have adverse long term consequences. Similarly, cash generating promotional activities offering incentives such as money-off coupons for consumers, free gifts for buyers and distributors or bonuses for salespeople may achieve a short term sales response but not permanent gain. Careful planning and monitoring of cash flow minimises constraints on the company's activities and avoids either panic measures or idle cash.

Flow of funds in manufacturing company

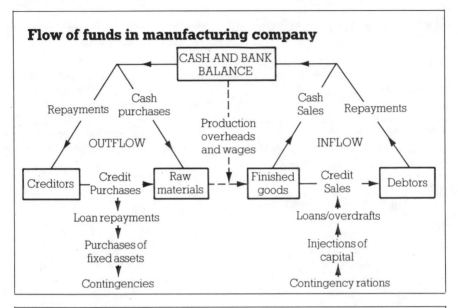

CASH BUDGET

	OCTOBER	NOVEMBER	DECEMBER
CASH INFLOW			
Payments from debtors	£100000	£120000	£140000
Cash sales	2000	2000	2000
	102000	122000	142000
CASH OUTFLOW			
Materials	40000	60000	70000
Wages/commission	9900	10350	10750
Departmental overheads and expenses	18620	13080	13820
New plant/machinery	42000	9000	10000
Repayment of debts	4000	4000	4000
Taxation	—	100000	—
Dividends	—	—	20000
	114520	196430	128570
NET CASH MOVEMENT	(12520)	(74430)	13430
Opening bank balance	81750	69230	(5200)
CLOSING BANK BALANCE	69230	(5200)	8230

Despite the large cash surplus at the end of October, the company will require extra funds by the end of November unless the pattern of receipts and payments can be altered (for instance, by delaying payments for fixed assets or suppliers' accounts).

How to make the most of your resources and increase cash flow

OBTAIN GENEROUS CREDIT FROM SUPPLIERS
Give bulk orders; adapt your order pattern to suit supplier; keep in touch and attempt amicable compromise: creditor likely to compromise for the sake of good business; do not send unsigned/undated/incorrect cheques or ignore statements; post dated cheques may keep creditors quiet if not too far ahead, but ensure you can meet debt on due date

GIVE LESS CREDIT TO CUSTOMERS
Tighten up your credit control policy in time/money terms; send pre-printed demands with statements; offer settlement discounts only where standard practice amongst the competition, since they may discourage reasonable settlement by your regular customers and they have a cost; debt collectors remove the burden of chasing debts but have few other uses and are expensive; use personal contact: demands by telephone or even in person, as well as those in writing, convey seriousness; take further action, eg request goods returned, issue writ (very lengthy process), or serve notice under section 223 of Companies Act 1948 requiring payment within three weeks

STOCK CONTROL
Reduce stock levels by more efficient, quicker deliveries of finished goods, and clearance of obsolete or excess stock

INCREASE PROFITS
Material utilisation: check spoilage rates, tolerance levels, inefficient scrap recovery
Production costs: check reject rates, machine breakdown incidence
Production planning and control: check labour utilization, work in progress levels, availability of tools/materials when needed, scheduling of orders to factory, adequate balance of seasonal/non-seasonal production
Warehousing/distribution: check delivery performance, breakage rates, packaging costs, transport and maintenance costs
Sales: check utilization of salespeople, amount of unnecessary paperwork, order processing delays, advertising
Budgetary control
Cost cutting incentives
Rationalization

REDUCE TAXATION
The simplest method of avoiding corporation tax is to write down the value of stocks as far as possible. However, extreme undervaluing of stocks equals evasion, which is illegal.

SALE AND LEASEBACK
Dispose of freehold premises and occupy same on long lease.

SELL FIXED ASSETS
Dispose of surplus land, premises.

SELL NON-PROFITABLE SECTIONS OF THE COMPANY

Exercises

1 Examine the ways in which your organization, your department and you handle the planning and control of cash flow. Talk to the finance manager and then to your colleagues. How often are you aware of cash flow crises? Are emergencies handled as they arise or is there any contingency planning? Are cash budgets prepared?

2 Examine your department's approaches to resources using the checklist on the previous page and make a list of possible areas for improvement. Involve *all* members of your department in understanding the need for maximizing the use of resources: note down ways in which you could do this for each group of people.

3 Prepare a cash budget for your personal domestic affairs for the next six months.

Further reading

HAZEL A C & REID A S. *Enjoying a Profitable Business*. London, Business Books Ltd, 1971

HARVEY D A & NETTLETON M. *Management Accounting*. London, Mitchell Beazley Publishers, 1983 (Core Business Studies)

JENNER P. *Your Business Problems Solved*. Newton Abbott, Devon, David and Charles (Publishers) Ltd, 1979

WOOD F & TOWNSLEY J. *Managerial Accounting and Finance*. Stockport, Cheshire, Polytech Publishers Ltd, 1983

And finally . . .

The Boston Consultancy Group's business portfolio matrix has four categories of products, each representing a distinct type of cash flow situation:

Stars: currently high cash users and high cash generators; will eventually become Cash Cows

Cash Cows: cash generators

Problem Children: large cash users, but may have potential

Dogs: Low cash generators with little potential

Product strategies should aim to turn Problem Children into Stars, and Stars into Cash Cows (and to dispose of Dogs), with a balance of products at each stage of development in its life cycle.

Statements on the source and application of funds (expressed either as cash or working capital) are required as part of large companies' audited accounts. These are sometimes known as "where got, where gone" statements. They provide guidance to creditors, shareholders and managers by focussing attention on the ways in which the company has raised funds and used them.

50 Reading the balance sheet

Every balance sheet is a snapshot of the financial structure of the business at a given time, disclosing the property and possessions of the business together with its internal and external debts and obligations. The balance sheet can, therefore, provide the manager with much useful information, and is a basis for analysis in understanding the strengths and weaknesses of the whole business. Together with the company's profit and loss (or income) statement, the balance sheet may help managers assess an organization's efficiency, draw conclusions about the effects of past decisions, and aid decision-making for future activities. Figures may be compared with those in earlier statements, with those of competitors, or with those of the industry in general.

As previously indicated, the balance sheet is a financial statement of reckoning which reports a company's assets, capital and liabilities at a specific date. *Assets* are things owned by the company which are valuable because they have cost money. Assets may be classified as 'current' if it is intended to turn them into cash in the near future, usually the next 12 months. Examples are cash, bank balances, stock, work in progress and debtors. Alternatively, they may be 'fixed' if they are intended to be kept and used, and to provide benefit to the company in the medium or long term. Examples are land, buildings, plant, vehicles, equipment and fittings. Intangible assets which enhance the value of the business may sometimes be included as fixed assets, eg goodwill, patents, copyrights. The balance sheet expresses the fact that every asset held by the company has to be financed in some way, either by capital, or by loans and items to be paid off (liabilities). The *capital* of the company is the funds originally contributed by the proprietor or shareholders, plus the funds which have accrued by profit, interest or upwards evaluation of assets (reserves). The *liabilities* of the company are obligations and debts owing by the company and, again, can be classified into current and long term. Current liabilities are items which have to be paid off within 12 months of the balance sheet date, eg outstanding accounts, creditors, bank overdrafts, unpaid dividends, current taxes. Long term liabilities are long term loans to the company such as debentures, which are similar to building society loans.

Since the sources of finance (capital plus liabilities) must equal the assets, a change in one must be reflected by a change in the other. These two 'sides' of the balance sheet represent the same picture looked at from two different angles. Company balance sheets may, in fact, be set out in either a horizontal format, with assets on the right and sources of finance on the left, or in a vertical format which places assets, capital and liabilities beneath each other in various orders.

The balance sheet may not always be representative of the average position of the business, since it is a snapshot picture. In addition, qualitative considerations, such as quality of personnel, cannot be represented. Managers should, as usual, exercise their judgement as to the degree to which they utilize financial statements in any analysis of the business.

Balance sheet (simplified)

Share capital (£1 shares)		*Fixed assets*		
Ordinary shares	100000	Land, buildings		
Preference shares (5%)	50000	etc at cost	498000	
		Aggregate		
Reserves		depreciation	(252000)	246000
Profit and Loss A/C	230000			
		Investments		28000
Mortgage debentures (7%)	112000			
		Current assets		
Current Liabilities		Stock in trade	172000	
Trade creditors	70000	Debtors and		
Bank overdrafts	3600.	prepayments	116000	
Current taxation	16400	90000	Cash	20000	308000
	582000			582000

Rules and principles in the preparation and publication of financial accounts

Financial accounting seeks to be objective, and there are rules laid down on the way in which activities of the business are recorded, known as accounting concepts. There are also approaches recommended to assist in the application of these concepts which are known as accounting conventions. Summaries of these concepts and conventions may be found in accounting textbooks. Many of them are the result of practice and pressures over a number of years, and the rules are sometimes modified from time to time (*see* comments on current cost accounting (CCA) in the final notes).

The Accounting Standards Committee produces Statements of Standard Accounting Practice (SSAPs) which also lay down rules regarding publication and disclosure for limited companies together with schedules contained in various Companies Acts (especially those of 1948, 1967 and 1981). Some of these are legal obligations, but sole traders, partnerships and companies beneath a certain size (measured by turnover, assets or numbers of employees) may be exempt.

Internal accounts, of course, may be produced in any form without recourse or reference to any accepted rules or requirements.

Users of balance sheets

The general theme of accounting information is that it should satisfy the needs of users in an objective manner. Users may include:

Owners, investors and shareholders who are interested in information about the return on, and the safety of, their investments;

Lenders and trade creditors who use the information to assess the company's liquidity (ability to pay off short term debts) and the safety of their claims on the company;

Trades unions and employees who are also interested in profitability, job prospects and the company's ability to finance wage claims;

The government and related bodies who are interested in information on profits, prices and the economy in general;

and of course, management . . .

Managerial analysis of the balance sheet

Examination of the balance sheet focuses mainly on capital structure and working capital; the excess of current assets over current liabilities. Many of the issues below are questions, not for the accountant who has prepared the balance sheet, but for the manager to raise.

Are assets fully utilized and not overvalued?

What action is being taken regarding old or obsolete equipment? Is it being sold off as scrap or is it being left idle, thus decreasing the earning power of capital?

Is there a sensible balance between the various items of current assets (stock, debtors, cash, etc)?

Is there too much money tied up in stock? Are stock levels too high in proportion to sales, or too low thus losing business? Is this stock position abnormal or average?

Is there an undesirable increase in debtors totals? Have the credit facilities offered to customers changed?

Is the amount of assets held as cash or in the current bank account too high. What is the daily cash transaction control system? Is enough being placed into higher interest accounts?

Is the amount of working capital adequate to run the business without undue strain? Are creditors paid on time, taking advantage of any cash discounts offered? Is the business able to take advantage of profitable activities that may suddenly occur, such as the bulk purchase of discounted goods?

Have the levels of working capital changed significantly over time? How do they compare with other similar businesses? Have they kept pace with inflation and company growth?

What are the levels of debt in relation to capital? How do these compare with industry averages? These are available from organizations such as the Centre for Inter-Firm Comparisons.

Exercises

1 Get hold of your company's most recently published balance sheet. Use it to examine the capital structure and working capital of the business, using the questions listed previously.

2 Discuss with colleagues your understanding of the messages contained in the balance sheet. Do you believe this to be an average representation, or were there particular factors in the period just preceding the preparation of the figures which might have caused distortion?

3 Does your company have a corporate view on current cost accounting?

4 Prepare a balance sheet showing your own personal assets and sources of finance.

Further reading

HARVEY D A & NETTLETON M. *Management Accounting*. London, Mitchell Beazley, 1983 (Core Business Studies)
ROBSON A P. *Essential Accounting for Managers*. 3rd ed. London, Cassell, 1970
WOOD F. *Business Accounting 1 and 2*. 3rd ed. Harlow, Essex, Longman, 1979 and 1980

And finally . . .

For many years, the concept of historic cost has been taken for granted in the preparation of financial accounts, so that assets have normally been shown at their historic acquisition cost. However, high inflation in recent years has focussed attention on methods of accounting which recognize changing price levels, thus reflecting more accurately the value of the business. SSAP 16, produced by the Accounting Standards Committee in 1980, required large companies to provide a second balance sheet alongside the conventional historic cost one, to reflect current cost accounting approaches. Companies with assets exceeding £2.5m, with a turnover of more than £5m, or with more than 250 employees are now required to produce both types of accounts. Current cost accounting is *not*, in fact, a system of accounting which reflects a reduction in the value of money resulting from *all* price increases, but is concerned only with changes in the price of *specific* assets in the business.

51 Productivity measures

The concept of productivity means different things to different people. It means the utilization of materials and machinery to the production engineer, of labour to the economist, and of capital to the accountant. In fact, productivity involves the effective use of all the above factors of production; each has to be balanced with the others to obtain the greatest output for the least possible consumption of resources.

All managers are responsible for the effectiveness of the operations within their authority, and the job of monitoring and increasing the productive use of resources is one of their principal functions. Even if they do not have direct control of capital equipment, they will have responsibility for people and materials. The manager will need to set objectives for each resource, and have some means of measuring productivity to compare with these objectives. Only when some attempt is made to quantify productivity levels can any improvements be made. Without measurement, managers run the risk of focussing attention on visible but insignificant problem areas, with the possibility of neglecting the more fundamental but less obvious areas of inefficiency. Failure by an engineering-oriented top management to monitor marketing activities, for example, may cause long term damage to the company's prospects.

Improvements in productivity do not only come from technological advance, although a new machine with a tenfold increase in output over the machine it replaces will clearly increase productivity of both machine and labour. The change may not be productive overall, however, if the substitution of labour by capital reduces the productivity of capital as measured by, say, the ratio of capital investment to production capacity.

There is also the difficult problem of measuring the productivity of labour in jobs in which output involves more than just a visible product. Where toil and sweat is replaced by planning and knowledge, achievement levels become much harder to define. What, for example, is the best way to measure the productivity of the sales representative, the design engineer, the company trainer, the research scientist or (probably the least analyzed of activities) the departmental manager? The absence of an instant answer to these questions makes the task of managing the productivity of the knowledge worker much more demanding.

The traditional measures of productivity are being supplemented increasingly by the use of complex, integrated productivity models, which combine several ratios to arrive at a single measure of efficiency for the whole department or organization and which take into account the balanced utilization of all the company's resources. These models are individually designed and remain closely guarded secrets, available only to the organizations for whom they were composed and who pay for their use.

Whether used as indicators of departmental efficiency, or for inter-firm comparison, productivity measures of any description need to be used with care. Many ratios are open to manipulation or inconsistency in their calculation, and conclusions may be misleading or over-simplified.

Types of productivity measures

The productivity objective: to maximize resource utilization and minimize loss or waste. Productivity may be expressed in physical or financial terms.

Resource	*Productivity measured by*
Machinery: equipment, buildings, tools	Output or throughput per machine hour Proportion of time used over total available time Per cent capacity utilized Per cent space utilization Per cent idle time Per cent machine cost over total cost
Materials: items consumed or converted by the system	Output or throughput per unit produced Per cent or quantity wastage, loss or scrap Per cent or quantity rework or rectification Per cent material cost over total cost
Labour	Output or throughput per man hour Added value per total number of employees Proportion of productive time over total available time Per cent capacity utilization Per cent idle time Per cent labour cost over total cost
Capital	Return on investment: the ratio of operating profit to operating assets indicates the overall efficiency of the operation Net profit margin: the ratio of operating profit to sales indicates the ability of the organization to generate profit from sales Asset turnover: the ratio of sales to operating assets indicates the company's ability to generate sales from its operating assets

Types of productivity measures/ continued

The productivity objective can and should be applied to all activities within the organization. The following describes measures which may be used in the marketing function:

Sales force	Number of calls per salesperson per day Average revenue per call Average cost per call Per cent orders per 100 calls Number of new and lost customers per period Per cent salesforce cost over total sales
Advertising campaign	Advertising cost per 1,000 people reached Per cent audience reached Number of enquiries stimulated Cost per enquiry Per cent attitude change

Other factors affecting productivity
(Qualitative rather than quantitative)

		Maximize productivity by examination of:
Knowledge	Can be expensive or unproductive if wrongly applied or under-utilized	Training, job specification, personal abilities
Time	Idle or wasted time, or undue pressure, affects productivity of people and machines	Working practices, demarcation, shift systems, quality of tools and environment
Process mix	Maximize use of the company's abilities, experience and reputation in its total activities.	Make or buy decisions, own or contracted labour, product mix, diversification.
Organization structure	Clear role definition results in less wasted effort; maximize use of all knowledge resources; motivation and achievement are important	Job descriptions, task setting, personnel policies.

Adapted from Drucker, P F. *Management: Tasks, Responsibilities, Practices (op. cit.)*

Exercises

1   Make a list of all the resources available in your department or section under the headings capital, labour and physical resources. How many of these are currently monitored?

2   Draft a note to your boss suggesting the greater use of productivity measures in specified areas, explaining why you believe these to be important.

3   Examine your own productivity as a manager. Express this as an objective or several objectives, in as precise a form as possible.

Further reading

DRUCKER P F. *Management: Tasks, Responsibilities, Practices*. London, Wm Heinemann, 1974

HARVEY D A & NETTLETON M. *Management Accounting*. London, Mitchell Beazley, 1983 (Core Business Studies)

KOTLER P. *Marketing Management: Analysis, Planning and Control*. 4th ed. Englewood Cliffs, NJ, Prentice Hall, 1980

WILD R. *Production and Operations Management: Principles and Techniques*. Eastbourne, Sussex, Holt, Rinehart and Winston Ltd, 1980

And finally . . .

Drucker comments that "we need a concept of productivity that considers together all the efforts that go into output and expresses them in relation to their result". Many of the most important opportunities for increasing productivity in the future lie beyond the traditional concept of manual workers tending machines. They lie in the areas of so-called non productive labour such as supervisors, maintenance workers and quality controllers, and within resources previously labelled as overheads such as researchers, planners, managers and innovators.